21st Century Architecture
APARTMENT LIVING

21st Century Architecture
APARTMENT LIVING

images
Publishing

Published in Australia in 2011 by
The Images Publishing Group Pty Ltd
ABN 89 059 734 431
6 Bastow Place, Mulgrave, Victoria 3170, Australia
Tel: +61 3 9561 5544 Fax: +61 3 9561 4860
books@imagespublishing.com
www.imagespublishing.com

Copyright © The Images Publishing Group Pty Ltd 2011
The Images Publishing Group Reference Number: 971

All rights reserved. Apart from any fair dealing for the purposes
of private study, research, criticism or review as permitted under
the Copyright Act, no part of this publication may be reproduced,
stored in a retrieval system or transmitted in any form by any
means, electronic, mechanical, photocopying, recording or otherwise,
without the written permission of the publisher.

National Library of Australia Cataloguing-in-Publication entry:

Title:	21st century architecture apartment living / edited by Beth Browne.
ISBN:	9781864704457 (hbk.)
Subjects:	Apartments—Design and construction. Architecture—21st century.
Other Authors/Contributors:	Browne, Beth.
Dewey Number:	728.314

Pre-publishing services by United Graphic Pte Ltd, Singapore

Printed on 140 gsm Chinese Matt Art paper by Paramount Printing Company Limited
Hong Kong

IMAGES has included on its website a page for special notices in relation to this and its
other publications. Please visit www.imagespublishing.com.

Contents

6	3 Mews Dwellings	ODOS architects
10	15 Central Park West	D'Aquino Monaco Inc.
14	59th Street Penthouse	Mojo Stumer Associates, p.c.
18	Apartment 65	Isay Weinfeld Architect
22	Apartment K	Atelier Peter Ebner and friends
26	Architect's Apartment	Peter Kuczia
30	Attico Apartment	Damilanostudio Architects
34	Bell Penthouse	Charles Rose Architects
38	Beverley Street Condo	Reigo & Bauer
42	Blur Loft	Johnsen Schmaling
46	Bonanova	marià castelló + josé antonio molina saiz, arquitectes
50	Bondi Penthouse	BMA
54	Breck Loft	McIntosh Poris Associates
58	Bulletin	Stanic Harding
62	CAP Apartment	Caprioglio Associati Studio di Architettura
66	Capri Apartment	gbc architetti
70	Carr Apartment	Craig Steely Architecture
74	Collector's Loft	UNStudio
78	Fifth Avenue Townhouse	Mojo Stumer Associates, p.c.
82	FILC Apartment	Caprioglio Associati Studio di Architettura
86	Harbour's Edge	Hulena Architects Ltd
90	Highpoint	Adam Richards Architects
94	Humelegården Apartment	Tham & Videgård Arkitekter
98	Kent Street Apartment	RLD
102	LC Apartment	Damilanostudio Architects
106	Ludwig Penthouse	Craig Steely Architecture
110	Manhattan Apartment	Mojo Stumer Associates, p.c.
114	The Mansion on Peachtree	Harrison Design Associates
118	Maria Borges Apartment	Atelier Bugio Arquitectura
122	Melbourne Apartment	fmd architects
126	Milsons Point	Stanic Harding
130	Mini Loft	OFIS Arhitekti
134	New York Apartment	Zivkovic Connolly Architects
138	Norman Reach Penthouse	RLD
142	One Rincon Hill	Carver + Schicketanz Architects
146	Organic Space	MoHen Design International
150	Pacific Heights Apartment	Seidel Architects
154	Parks Residence	Eggleston | Farkas Architects
158	Playroom Apartment	Caprioglio Associati Studio di Architettura
162	Pyrmont	Stanic Harding
166	Quant 1	Ippolito Fleitz Group – Identity Architects
170	Riverside Drive	D'Aquino Monaco Inc.
174	Rosas Apartment	57STUDIO | Architects
178	S	Ippolito Fleitz Group – Identity Architects
182	The SCH	Ippolito Fleitz Group – Identity Architects
186	Seafront Apartment	Architecture Project
190	SF Apartment	Caprioglio Associati Studio di Architettura
194	Shuwai	MoHen Design International
198	Spring Street Apartment	Rice Design
202	St. Louis Art House	Charles Rose Architects
206	St. Ursula Street Apartment	Architecture Project
210	Transparent Loft	Olson Kundig Architects
214	TriBeCa Loft	Mojo Stumer Associates, p.c.
218	Urban Condominium	Bohlin Cywinski Jackson
222	Index of Architects	

3 Mews Dwellings

DUBLIN, IRELAND   **ODOS architects**

Credits: Casey O'Rourke Associates (engineers)

Floor area: 190 square metres / 2045 square feet

Program: New build of three apartments on a mews laneway

Ceiling height/s: 2.5 metres / 8 feet

Rooms: Three bedrooms, ensuite, family bathroom, den/theatre-room/garage, living, kitchen/dining, home office, external terraces/decks

Ventilation: Natural ventilation from operable window sections and wall vents; bathrooms mechanically ventilated

Sound attenuation: Wall insulation, acoustic floor matting and externally mounted air-to-water heat pump

Green features: A grey-water harvesting system and a boiler linked to an air-to-water heat pump maximise the use of renewable energy—all external courtyards drain to this grey-water harvesting system located below the upper courtyard to the rear of each dwelling in order to feed the irrigation systems for the gardens, toilets and washing machines

A flexible pattern of built and unbuilt spaces stitched together by a central circulation route formed the design basis for three split-level apartments. Across seven floor plates in total, unbuilt or 'trapped' spaces form a series of outdoor rooms, bringing the experience of landscape and foliage into the core of each dwelling and stimulating a strong spatial dialogue between opposing areas.

The gardens vary in orientation and ensure every room has direct access to natural daylight and ventilation. They also play host to a variety of plant species, ensuring a colourful and scented environment year round. At night, the lighting strategy for these external rooms provides a lit backdrop to the internal spaces and a variety of outlooks.

The splits or shifts in floor level allow easy connections between floor plates and swift navigation throughout each dwelling. They also afford a dual aspect to most of the spaces within each dwelling. As the sun moves during the day each space catches indirect sunlight from external rooms beyond.

The material palette in each dwelling, while minimal, offers abundant contrasts. Polished concrete floors are set against soft velvet curtains and voiles. Warm black-stained timber is juxtaposed with the green foliage in the courtyards. A white pebbled courtyard floor contrasts with warm black rendered walls. Internal and external timber fins offer obscured views while the frameless glazed openings offer unimpeded views. Solid walls work in conjunction with open balustrading and mirrored walls, both internally and externally, to create reflections and cast shadows.

PHOTOGRAPHY: Barbara Corsico

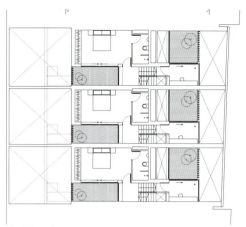

Third floor plan

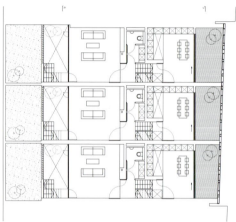

Second floor plan

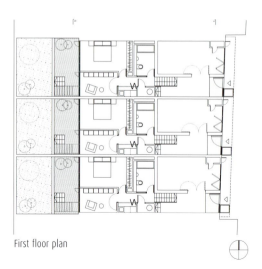

First floor plan

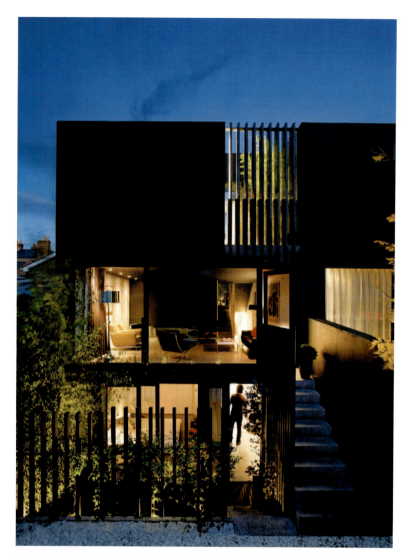

15 Central Park West

NEW YORK CITY, NEW YORK, UNITED STATES **D'Aquino Monaco Inc.**

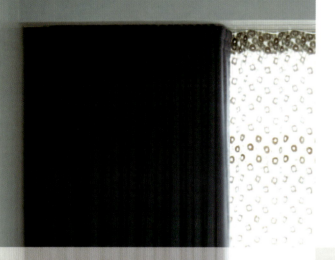

Floor area: 325 square metres / 3500 square feet

Program: Interior design and architectural remodelling of an existing apartment

Ceiling height/s: 3 metres / 10 feet

Rooms: Gallery, living, library/dining, family room, three bedrooms with ensuite bathrooms, kitchen, breakfast room, laundry and powder room

Ventilation: Low-airspeed ceiling plenums

Sound attenuation: Floor and ceiling insulation, acoustically detached walls and acoustically heavily insulated mechanical equipment (also vibration insulated)

Green features: Good insulation, glass with low solar entrée and motor operated translucent screens for all windows

The focus of the interior design and architecutral remodelling of this apartment on Central Park West was style and colour. The clients were seeking a varied experience with memorable rooms. By eliminating service corridors and rearranging the kitchen the designers created a spacious backdrop for a new collection of modern art and fine furnishings.

The project became an artistic dialogue between the designers, their clients and a number of artisans. The foyer mouldings were created in collaboration with designers Moss & Lam to establish a sculptural identity for the entrance, removing all traces of the original prewar-style crown moulding. This set the tone and style for the apartment, blending 20th century Italian and French antiques with modern sculptural artworks.

A sculpture by Richard Artschwager that was originally intended for the wall became a ceiling piece in the family room, and is balanced by a gravity-defying storage wall on chrome springs that was created by the designers. In a similar manner, a sensuous Lucite sculpture by Jim Shaw doubles as a unique coffee table in the living room. The designers' love for all things 1940s, particularly Italian designs from this period, is expressed in the extensive use of Fornasetti wallpaper in the kitchen, breakfast room and laundry. Although each room is unique, a playful dialogue between art and design brings the apartment together as a whole.

PHOTOGRAPHY: Peter Murdoch

59th Street Penthouse

NEW YORK CITY, NEW YORK, USA **Mojo Stumer Associates, p.c.**

Floor area: 420 square metres / 4500 square feet

Program: Renovation of an existing penthouse apartment

Ceiling height/s: 4.2 metres / 14 feet

Rooms: Two bedrooms with full baths, kitchen, formal living, den, powder room, two office suites, casual dining and large entry foyer

Although the footprint of this penthouse provided many options for delineating the space, a free-flowing floor plan was decided on, moving away from the segregated spaces of the original layout.

The clients wanted the apartment to be able to accommodate their formal Broadway show premiere functions as well as provide a relaxed living environment. To meet this need, moveable wall partitions of glass and stainless steel were incorporated to create separate spaces when required. It was also important that each new element complemented the sweeping, floor-to-ceiling, 360-degree Manhattan views. From the bathrooms to the bedrooms, this was of fundamental importance.

The interior detailing is sleek and contemporary without sacrificing comfort. The clients wanted the very best quality hard materials and the latest designs the world had to offer in furniture and soft materials. The material palette is thus a combination of many striking elements, including Makassar ebony, Dupioni silk, alpaca wool, Lima limestone, shagreen and basalt. These materials combine with the grand architecture and beautiful craftsmanship in symphonic style.

PHOTOGRAPHY: Paul Warchol

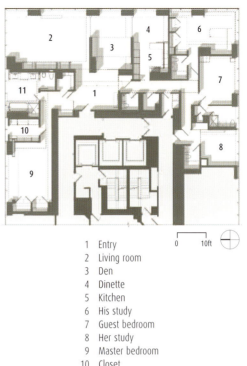

1   Entry
2   Living room
3   Den
4   Dinette
5   Kitchen
6   His study
7   Guest bedroom
8   Her study
9   Master bedroom
10 Closet
11 Master bathroom

Apartment 65

NEW YORK CITY, NEW YORK, USA **Isay Weinfeld Architect**

This apartment—located in a historic building in Manhattan—was completely remodeled to accommodate four bedrooms, an office, a large living room, a dining room and other service and supporting facilities.

The entry hall is minimalist in style—clad entirely with wood—and features two wood benches and a pair of lamps designed by Jean Royère.

Beyond the entry an all-white hallway leads to the dining room on the left, where a vintage crystal lamp hangs above an oval 1950s Danish dining table and chairs designed by Sergio Rodrigues. To the right of the hallway is the living room, featuring two distinct sitting areas—one somewhat informal with an L-shaped sofa and a large television; and the other not exactly formal, but offering a more sober atmosphere.

The hallway walls are white-painted wood panel concealing not only a built-in bar, but also the doors to the children's and guest bedrooms and the office. The main bedroom and the nursery are accessible from the sitting room.

PHOTOGRAPHY: 2011 © photo@leonardofinotti.com

Credits: Isay Weinfeld (architect), Domingos Pascali (collaborating architect), Monica Cappa (project manager) and Leandro Garcia (design team)

Floor area: 410 square metres / 4410 square feet

Program: Complete remodel of an apartment to accommodate four bedrooms and additional living and service spaces

Ceiling height/s: 2.5 metres / 8 feet

Rooms: Four bedrooms, office, living room, dining room, bar, hall, kitchen and service/support areas

Ventilation: Air-conditioning and heating system

Green features: Translucent screens for all windows for efficient temperature control

1 Kitchen
2 Dining
3 Playroom
4 Bedroom
5 Hall
6 Walk-in robe
7 Bar
8 Wine cellar
9 Office
10 Sitting/living
11 TV room

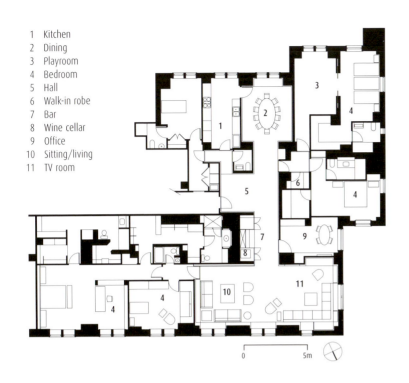

OBERÖSTERREICH, AUSTRIA

Apartment K

Atelier Peter Ebner and friends

This apartment is located in a multi-storey residential house that was built in the 1950s. Despite the small floor area—just 75 square metres—the apartment now enjoys an unexpected generosity of space and comfortably accommodates a family of five.

The design is based on the idea of conserving all of the available space in one single volume. Rather than dividing the space into separate rooms, each with a mono-functional use, room-defining furniture has been placed in the centre of the volume and can be opened in every direction. This furniture is part of the room but it also forms a 'room within a room', combining several different functions in one centrepiece. The integrated kitchen can be hidden completely behind a folding wall element, the dining table swings out of the wall cladding, the seating bench transforms into a bed and the partition door between the children's and the parents' rooms conceals a private office.

The walls, floor and ceiling have been painted with a botanical pattern by Austrian artist Rainer Füreder of Linz, giving the inhabitants the impression of moving through a surreal landscape reminiscent of Henri Rousseau, which blurs the real edges of the geometrical space.

PHOTOGRAPHY: Margerita Spiluttini

Floor area: 75 square metres / 800 square feet

Program: Renovation and remodel of an unremarkable two-bedroom apartment into a stylish loft for five occupants

Ceiling height/s: 3 metres / 10 feet

Rooms: A single room with different zones for bedrooms, kitchen, dining and living (each zone can be closed off or opened up to use the full floor area)

Ventilation: Floor heating and natural ventilation

Sound attenuation: Sliding wall screens made of felt

Green features: Heavily insulated glass

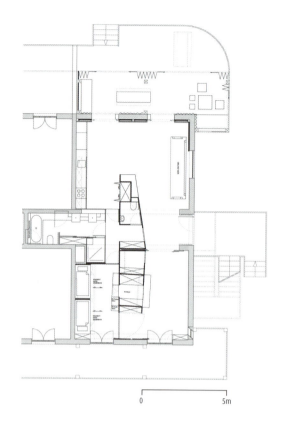

0   5m

Architect's Apartment

OSNABRÜCK, GERMANY   **Peter Kuczia**

For over 100 years this attic above two apartments in the centre of Osnabrück was vacant, serving as a storage room, until the architect recreated the space as his own apartment.

His design focused on crafting a comfortable living space while reducing construction and lifecycle costs. The existing wooden roof structure was retained and supplemented by new roofing, walls and dormers. A newly constructed roof terrace offers a lovely view of the city.

The energy-efficient geometric shape of the saddleback roof—its volume maximised beneath a relatively small outer skin—reduces heat loss. Higher-than-normal levels of thermal insulation and the benefits of passive solar heating gained via skylights also help to ensure the apartment is very energy efficient.

The original brick walls of the attic and old chimneys have been left uncovered to act as passive energy buffers. The new walls were constructed with gypsum board, with some forming built-in furniture—particularly in the functional-wing, which includes a wardrobe, storage space and a bathroom. Situated in the central zone of the apartment, it forms a cube with a small open gallery above.

PHOTOGRAPHY: Agata Kuczia

Floor area: 175 square metres / 1880 square feet

Program: Reconstruction of an attic (built in 1905) into an apartment

Ceiling height/s: 0–5.5 metres / 0–18 feet (droop)

Rooms: Two bedrooms, two bathrooms, open kitchen and living room with dining and lounge seating areas, study and storage room

Ventilation: Natural ventilation, gas-condensing boiler and radiators for heating

Sound attenuation: Floor and ceiling insulation and acoustically detached walls

Green features: Energy-efficient geometric shape, very good thermal insulation, heat-insulating glass, passive and active use of solar energy and reuse of existing wooden roof structure

1 Entry
2 Kitchen
3 Living
4 Bedroom
5 Nursery
6 Bathroom
7 Laundry
8 Study
9 Roof deck

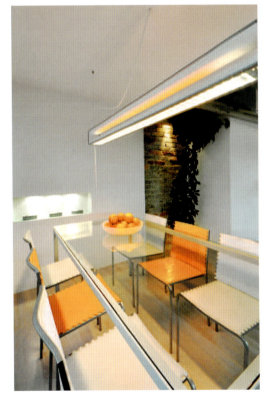

Attico Apartment

CUNEO, PIEMONTE, ITALY **Damilanostudio Architects**

Floor area: 240 square metres / 2500 square feet

Program: Refurbished attic apartment

Ceiling height/s: 2.7 metres / 9 feet

Rooms: Entrance, study, living, dining, kitchen, closet, bathroom, master bedroom, master bathroom

Ventilation: Natural ventilation directly integrated with a mechanical ventilation system

Sound attenuation: Walls are two sheets of plasterboard with a mineral wool panel interposed, the air-handling unit is placed under the roof to reduce noise and the floor is insulated from impact noise by horizontal dividers

Green features: Triple glazing with low-E coating and argon gas

The brief for this project was to expand the space of an attic that, despite being quite large, appeared cramped due to a pitched roof that was compressing its volume. The final result is a bright, spacious and dynamic apartment that perfectly reflects the owner's needs.

Converting attics into apartments can be problematic as the reduced room at the ridge of the roof requires customised spaces. For this apartment the architect chose to create large rooms with few dividing walls in order to impart a sense of breadth to the apartment.

A section of the wall near the main door was removed to create a window in the ceiling. This skylight causes a column of light to fall gracefully onto a grand piano, immediately catching the eye of everyone who enters the apartment.

The sleeping area is designed as an independent space—an alcove to retire to at the end of the day. The bed and the bathtub, separated by glass, are in constant communication with each other, while soft light dampens the rigid geometry of the room. Within the bathroom—the only enclosed room in the apartment—the shower is placed at the cockloft level to exploit its height.

The interior colours and materials were chosen to breathe air and life into the apartment. Reflective white floors create a homogeneous surface that complements funiture of chestnut wood and facing of Indian stone.

PHOTOGRAPHY: Andrea Martiradonna

Bell Penthouse

NEW YORK CITY, NEW YORK, USA **Charles Rose Architects**

Floor area: 370 square metres / 4000 square feet

Program: A penthouse combining private living space and public performance space for a professional musician

Ceiling height/s: Between 3.2 metres and 6.7 metres (atrium) / 10 feet 6 inches and 22 feet (atrium)

Rooms: Atrium open to the living room, dining room, eat-in kitchen, library/study area, mezzanine balcony connecting to the terrace, master bedroom and bathroom

Ventilation: Ventilation is provided by a high-velocity system with air vents incorporated into the lighting design

Sound attenuation: Sound separation for the lower floor was augmented with an 8-centimetre (3-inch) slab and triple-glazed windows on the street façade are noise dampening

Green features: Low-E thermopane glass with UV filter, LED lighting fixtures and good insulation

This two-storey penthouse for virtuoso violinist Joshua Bell was designed not only as a residential space for the musician, but as a performance space as well. In addition to the living areas, the penthouse includes a terrace with seating areas and a spa. At the client's request, the violin's form and materials became an aesthetic reference point for the project, and a specifically designed folded ceiling enhances the acoustics for the owner's 300-year-old Gibson Stradivarius.

The penthouse sits atop a 1910 industrial building. The open, loft-like space expresses a physical reinterpretation of the musical instrument the artist has come to master. The work is sculptural and lyrical. The top two floors of the building were gutted and restructured. The open interior is dominated by a glass and oxidised steel staircase leading to a mezzanine balcony above the living area. Outside, the terrace evokes a pagan outdoor spa with a hot tub and shower open to the sky, a trellised pergola, a fireplace and a copper-clad chimney. Natural light pours through the double-storey interior via the lofty atrium.

The evocation of the violin is evident throughout. The grille patterns in the cabinet doors resemble abstracted *f*-holes, and the apartment's two dominating wood finishes—reclaimed bubinga for the floors and reclaimed wenge for the millwork—approximate the aged maple, ebony and spruce of the musician's beloved Stradivarius.

The wenge window seating in the living room doubles as storage for the owner's sheet-music collection, and in the kitchen serves as a banquette for the wenge-topped table designed by the architect. Connecting the living area and the dining area is a limestone and patinated steel fireplace. An oxidised-steel mantel cantilevers out on one end to double as a bar. Ideal for hosting guests, this area transforms into an intimate concert hall. A velvet curtain can be used to divide the library from the living area, functioning as a proscenium for Bell's bimonthly salons. In the master bedroom the architect carved out a window to frame, in its entirety, the Flatiron Building, which is much admired by the client.

PHOTOGRAPHY: Chuck Choi

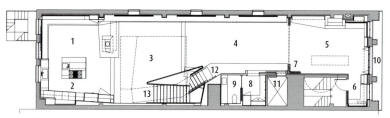

Upper floor plan

1	Dining	8	Coat room
2	Kitchen	9	Powder room
3	Living	10	Balcony
4	'Recital' Hall	11	Elevator
5	Library/studio	12	Stair to mezzanine and roof terrace
6	Office		
7	'Proscenium' curtain	13	Stair to lower level

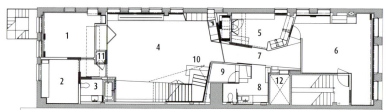

Lower floor plan

1	Guest room	6	Master bedroom
2	Study	7	Hall
3	Guest bathroom	8	Master bathroom
4	Media room	9	Tub/shower
5	Dressing room	10	Stair to upper level
		11	Washer/dryer
		12	Elevator

Beverley Street Condo

TORONTO, CANADA **Reigo & Bauer**

Credits: JH Reynolds Contracting and O'Sullivan Millwork

Floor area: 280 square metres / 3000 square feet

Program: One new apartment formed from two separate units

Ceiling height/s: 2.4 metres / 8 feet (entry, powder room, kitchen, master dressing room); 2.6 metres / 8.7 feet (guest suite, office, den, living, dining, master suite)

Rooms: Two bedrooms with ensuites; partially separated living, dining and kitchen/breakfast areas; office/den and four terraces

Ventilation: Large operable doors and windows on the north, west, and south sides of the apartment provide cross ventilation and heating and cooling is delivered by the apartment's own standalone forced-air system

Sound attenuation: Sound transmission between apartments is minimal and did not need to be addressed; within the apartment, acoustically compatible spaces were located in the same wing, whereas acoustically incompatible spaces were placed in opposite wings; a continuous translucent sheer provides 40 metres (135 feet) of soft, sound absorbing surface and both the master bedroom and guest bedroom have oversized fabric-wrapped headboards to absorb sound

Green features: Materials, paints and finishes were selected for their low environmental impact

Two units were joined together to create this unique 280-square-metre (3000-square-foot) apartment in downtown Toronto. The owners sought large spaces for entertaining as well as modestly scaled private rooms—a setting they could not find in existing apartments.

The newly created apartment has a U-shaped plan that snakes around the building's central corridor, creating an interior with three perimeter walls of floor-to-ceiling windows. A new 'ceilingscape' helps to seamlessly knit together the former units, along with the new wide-plank, black-oiled ash floors and 45 metres (150 feet) of continuous white sheers that float from hidden coves in the ceiling. The crisp contrast of the white walls and black floors acts to illuminate the interiors, with help from the glass partitions and strategic use of mirrors.

At the heart of the plan are the living room, dining room and kitchen. They are flanked at one end by the master suite and at the other by a freestanding volume with a glass wall that draws light into the den and the home office. A guest suite at the tip of the unit is accessed from a corridor on the other side of the den and office to offer total privacy.

Damask-patterned opalescent tile wraps around the kitchen's drop ceiling, glittering over units made from copper-mauve cupboards, charcoal-grey mirror walls and luminescent Corian counters. In the living room, traditional wingback chairs take on a modern twist upholstered in a juicy turquoise velour. A built-in bar is stylistically modern, but maintains old-world charm in polished mahogany. Perhaps the jewel of the apartment is the custom-designed dining room table surrounded by Arper swivel chairs in plum-coloured wool, enlivened by a playful light fitting—a mirror silhouette of a traditional-style chandelier.

The condo's private areas are softer and more sensuous. In the master suite, the unusually shaped dressing area, bedroom and bathroom are woven together by a luxurious palette of materials and textures. A glass partition separates the bedroom from the ensuite bathroom, inviting natural light that reflects off the gleaming Carrera marble walls and the white Corian box with a sunken tub. Black glass floor tile with wisps of copper makes a fashionable interplay with the more serious marble.

PHOTOGRAPHY: Tom Arban Photography

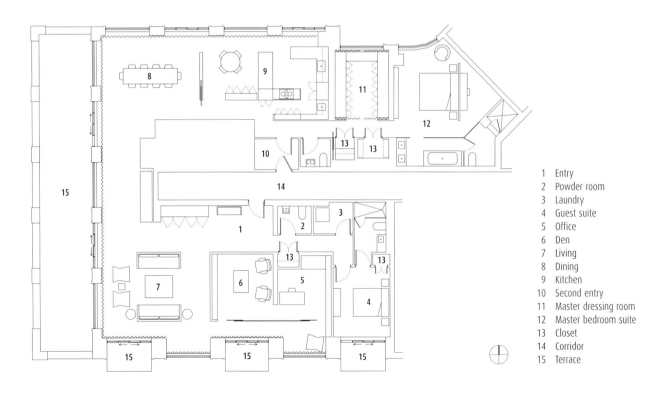

1 Entry
2 Powder room
3 Laundry
4 Guest suite
5 Office
6 Den
7 Living
8 Dining
9 Kitchen
10 Second entry
11 Master dressing room
12 Master bedroom suite
13 Closet
14 Corridor
15 Terrace

Blur Loft

MILWAUKEE, WISCONSIN, USA **Johnsen Schmaling**

Floor plan: 240 square metres / 2600 square feet

Program: Renovated apartment organised into three parallel zones

Ceiling height/s: 2.7 metres / 9 feet

Rooms: Master suite (master bedroom with bathroom and walk-in closet), two flexible spaces with shared bathroom (can be used as bedrooms, offices, or as expansion space for the living hall), open kitchen, dining space, living hall, winter garden (enclosed patio), balcony and powder room

Ventilation: Central air-conditioning system with air exchanger and automatic humidification

Sound attenuation: Sound-attenuating underlay and matting in flooring, RC-resilient channels and sound-insulating batt insulation

Green features: All glazing is high-efficiency, low-E and argon-filled; the winter garden, separated from the main living hall by sliding panels, serves as a thermal buffer for the unit; compact fluorescent lighting throughout, with LED cove lighting in living hall; low-flow plumbing fixtures for water conservation; high percentage of locally-sourced and rapidly renewable materials and fixtures, including tiles and flooring; and low-VOC paints and stains

The program of this urban residence—on the top floor of a former cold storage facility with commanding views of Milwaukee's skyline—was organised in three parallel zones. A long living hall, flooded with natural light and bracketed by an open kitchen on one end and a generous sunroom on the other, occupies the first, most public zone. Two narrow floor-to-ceiling cabinet towers anchor the linear space and incorporate storage, art niches, wine racks, and audiovisual equipment as well as the home's fireplace, while creating more intimate areas for dining, lounging and sitting.

The second zone is occupied by a series of flexible spaces separated from the living hall by 8-foot square translucent sliding panels that can be completely retracted. Depending on the position of the panels, these flexible rooms can be totally separated from the living hall or completely connected to it to serve either as private bedrooms, dens or media rooms, or to provide additional gathering space for larger social events. The translucent panels allow daylight to penetrate deep into the unit, illuminating areas that otherwise would have had no access to natural light. Conversely, the panels transform into enigmatic canvases when lit from behind, their blurred projections subtly revealing glimpses of life unfolding in the adjacent rooms.

The third spatial layer contains the home's most private functions, including a spacious master bathroom, walk-in closets, storage space and other back-of-the-house functions. 'Landlocked' deep inside the building because of existing plumbing shafts, the walls and floor of the cavernous bathroom space are lined with thin stacked-stone tiles, their horizontal format alluding to geological strata. In the centre of the bathroom, the floor plane folds up to create a raised plinth for the tub. Floating above the plinth, an open bamboo frame serves as the vanity and spatial device that organises the room into distinct but interconnected areas. Within the bamboo frame, a pair of suspended double-sided mirrors forms the backdrop for simple vessel sinks, altering the perception of the bathroom's actual boundaries, while allowing views to the other side of the space.

PHOTOGRAPHY: Doug Edmunds

1 Kitchen
2 Dining
3 Living
4 Winter garden
5 Master suite
6 Flexible space (bedroom/office/open to living)
7 Bathroom
8 Powder room
9 Balcony

Bonanova

BARCELONA, SPAIN **marià castelló + josé antonio molina saiz, arquitectes**

Credits: José Antonio Molia Saiz and Marià Castelló Martinez; Sonia Iben Jellal

Floor area: 240 square metres / 2600 square feet

Program: Apartment renovation for a family of six

Ceiling height/s: 2.6 metres / 8.5 feet

Rooms: Four bedrooms with ensuites, kitchen, dining and lounge areas, library, storage room and private garden area with exterior lounge

Ventilation: Low-airspeed ceiling plenum

Sound attenuation: Floor and ceiling insulation

Green features: Good insulation and south–north / east–west natural ventilation

The brief for this apartment located in a low-density part of the Bonanova quarter in Barcelona was to reorganise the existing functional program on the ground floor to suit the needs of a family with four children. Before the intervention the plan was highly fragmented with a poor relationship between the spaces. The modification has affected almost 100 percent of the floor area—the only pre-existing rooms that survived are the two bathrooms and the core for vertical communication. Everything else has been rearranged to allow more freedom in the structural system.

The resulting plan manifests in three strips parallel to the street frontage. The band closest to the street contains the main entrance with a large lobby and the children's bedrooms, each of which has an ensuite bathroom.

The second band, greater in size, contains the vertical communication core, the master bedroom and the public area of the house, which comprises the kitchen, dining room and lounge. All of these southwest-facing spaces have direct contact with the garden. The kitchen is designed to stay open and connected to the main volume, but can also be separated by a set of sliding doors when required.

In order to achieve greater harmony between the original substrate and the new design, a very limited palette of materials was employed. Essentially, it includes the restoration of the pre-existing solid pine floor; plaster coating in the partitions, ceilings and other vertical walls; water-resistant MDF board painted white for use as furniture; synthetic quartz plates in white and transparent laminated glass for the bathrooms and exposed concrete in the pillars of the existing structure.

PHOTOGRAPHY: Estudi EPDSE

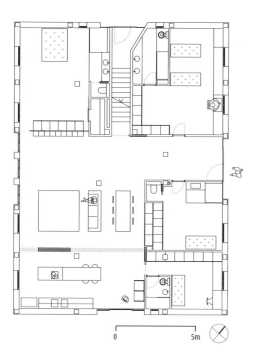

Bondi Penthouse

SYDNEY, NEW SOUTH WALES, AUSTRALIA **BMA**

Credits: Kevin Ng, Brian Meyerson, Sebastian Kaintoch, Amanda Ienco

Floor area: 215 square metres / 2300 square feet

Program: Conversion of vacant roof space into a beachside penthouse apartment

Ceiling height/s: 2.7 metres / 9 feet

Rooms: Three bedrooms with ensuites; open-plan kitchen, dining and living area; study nook off entry; separate sun terrace and architectural water feature along corridor leading from lift

Ventilation: ACTRON AIR SP Series 3.2-star-rated reverse cycle

Sound attenuation: Rubber underlay to structural steel footings to attenuate vibration, rubber underlay to internal timber flooring and acoustic insulation to lightweight internal walls

Green features: Bathrooms with operable skylights, insulated external walls and roof, 4-star-rated WC and photovoltaic cells on roof

In order to fulfil his vision of a beachside penthouse in the centre of iconic Bondi Beach, the owner of this apartment acquired the vacant roof space of a 1920s Art Deco building from the body corporate.

The architect's response was an addition with clean contemporary lines that presented a clear separation from the rest of the building. The minimal white aesthetic of the penthouse contrasts with the pastel blue of the existing building while addressing the council's stipulation that the addition should not be visible from the street.

The lightweight steel frame used to maintain the structural integrity of the existing building is clad in composite metallic façade panelling. This material was also used to clad the living area ceiling and hallway walls and to conceal the fireplace. Wide American oak floorboards and monolithic limestone slabs in the bathrooms give the interior a light and airy feel reminiscent of a beachside cottage.

External glazing was inclined outwards to continue the angular design theme and to minimise glass reflection inside. Sheer curtains are employed to contrast with the machined-metal surfaces and to add a dynamic element to the space. A floating glass bridge brings the water feature inside the house and contrasts with a summery beach-themed montage created by a local photographer, which lines the opposite wall.

The established locations of the lift and stair as well as the setback requirements underpinned the layout of the apartment. The floors are split level and the living and kitchen areas, which open out to an external terrace, are set on the higher level to take full advantage of the beach views. Bedrooms, all with adjoining ensuites and views to the beach, are located on the northern side. The corridor located on the south side is naturally lit via a 10-metre skylight running parallel to the water feature.

PHOTOGRAPHY: Brett Boardman

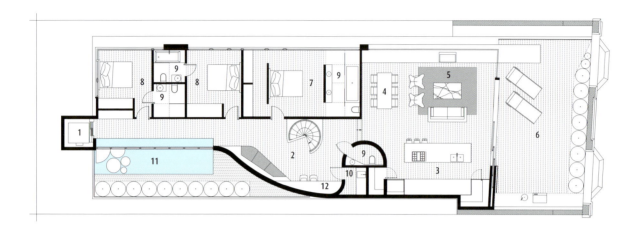

1 Lift
2 Entry foyer
3 Kitchen
4 Dining
5 Living
6 Outdoor terrace
7 Master bedroom
8 Bedroom
9 Bathroom
10 Laundry
11 Water feature
12 Study

Breck Loft

DETROIT, MICHIGAN, USA   **McIntosh Poris Associates**

In renovating this three-storey loft the architect made the best functional use of the existing vertical structure and kept the space relatively free of interior walls. Set within an exposed-brick wall in the living room, a large window/door system allows natural light to travel throughout as it bounces off the polished hardwood flooring and smooth wall surfaces before penetrating well into the dining and kitchen areas.

Because the architects supported the client's desire to maintain the integrity of the original piano warehouse, many of its existing features remain. Perpendicular to the brick wall in the living room, which extends into the master suite, a concrete wall was painted brown, giving it the appearance of patterned and textured wallpaper. Dark-stained millwork and steel are exposed at ceiling level throughout the loft, carrying the existing theme along.

Woodwork also features strongly in the master suite. From the dark-stained platform bed and four-panel wall system that affords privacy, to the maple nightstands and shelving unit, and the extensive wall-to-wall, floor-to-ceiling maple closet serviced by a 20-foot library ladder, the woodwork complements the hardwood flooring. Prior to renovation, part of this flooring was missing, so the architects replaced it with custom-distressed wood to blend with the existing floor.

Stainless steel is featured throughout the kitchen, including a steel-tiled wall behind the stove. An island matching the black granite counter tops was placed at the kitchen's centre to provide additional counter space. A set of three glass lanterns hangs over the bar, offering a soft glow. The cabinetry, island, and bar structures, including a built-in wine rack resting within the bar itself, are all made of oak.

The bathroom maintains the contemporary style of the loft by mixing a blend of dark-stained cabinetry, stainless steel, porcelain, ceramic tiles and glass. The steel hardware in the shower is visible through the glass walls and door and matches the fixtures throughout the space.

PHOTOGRAPHY: Kevin Bauman

Floor area: 140 square metres / 1500 square feet

Program: Renovation of a former piano warehouse into a modern, open loft dwelling

Ceiling height/s: The ceiling height slopes with the building roof from 5 metres / 16 feet, 8 inches (at the mezzanine) to 4.7 metres / 15 feet, 4 inches (at the living room and master bedroom)

Rooms: Two bedrooms (master suite and mezzanine bedroom), two bathrooms, living, kitchen, dining, office, roof deck

Ventilation: High-efficiency furnace and roof-mounted condenser for air conditioning, exposed ductwork in the loft and ceiling fans assist in distribution and recirculation of the air

Sound attenuation: Floors and wall-cavities are insulated and the air-handling unit is placed on the roof

Green features: Renovation and reuse of a vacant existing building, low-flow plumbing fixtures and energy-star appliances, high-efficiency water heater and furnace, salvaged pine flooring from a local source and passive cooling achievable by opening the windows and sliding doors at the main level and rooftop patio door

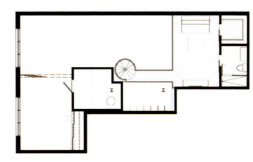

Mezzanine plan

First floor plan

Bulletin

SYDNEY, NEW SOUTH WALES, AUSTRALIA **Stanic Harding**

This project involved the interior fit out of the top of a new office building designed by PTW Architects near Circular Quay in Sydney. The building owner's original intention was to create one large, double-height penthouse on the top two levels. The architect's involvement resulted in two smaller double-storey apartments, both of which can be used as office space that is supported by living facilities on the upper level. One apartment was designed as the building owner's office and features a double-height space enclosed by a glazed box, while the other apartment was to be sold. The project also included the fit out of the lift lobby.

The lower level of each apartment accommodates an entry, secretarial space, waiting area, toilet, tea making facilities, the main office and an associated meeting area. The upper level is connected by a secret stair and accommodates a kitchen, dining area, living space, bathroom and single bedroom.

The aim was to produce quality apartments that would complement the Circular Quay location and meet the needs of business people requiring a business address in the city for a few days a week, as well as the functions of a serviced apartment.

PHOTOGRAPHY: Paul Gosney

Floor area: 400 square metres / 4300 square feet (over two levels)

Program: Fit out for a penthouse apartment in a new office building

Ceiling height/s: 2.6 metres / 8.5 feet

Rooms: Lower level: entry, secretarial space, waiting area, toilet and tea making facilities; upper level (connected by a secret stair): kitchen, dining, bathroom, living and bedroom

Ventilation: Operable external louvre system

Sound attenuation: Acoustic flooring

Green features: Sun blinds, recycled hardwood flooring for the residential level and intelligent lighting systems

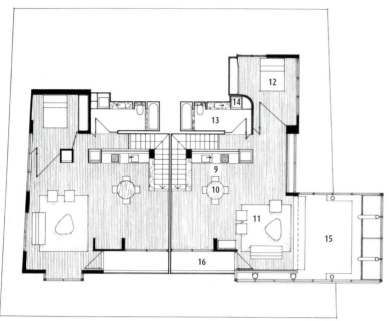
Upper floor plan

1 Lobby
2 Entry
3 Secretary
4 Waiting area
5 Tea/coffee room
6 Powder room
7 Office
8 Stairs
9 Kitchen
10 Dining
11 Living
12 Bedroom
13 Bathroom
14 Laundry
15 Void
16 Terrace

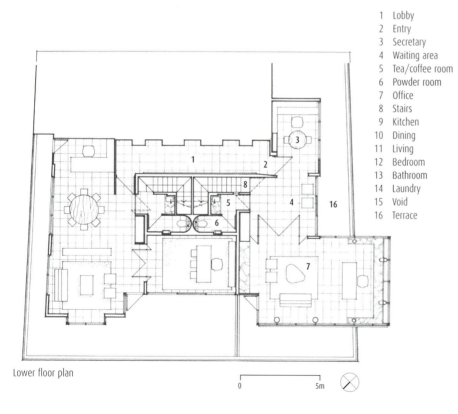
Lower floor plan

CAP Apartment

MESTRE, ITALY **Filippo Caprioglio – Caprioglio Associati Studio di Architettura**

The design approach for this transformation arose from a desire to display, in a living space that was as open as possible, a large number of paintings, sculptures, books and industrial design objects.

The large linear library defines the various areas within the apartment; most of which are are continuous, but subdivided by function. A curved wall, dynamically defined in the connected space, separates private and public areas.

White is used as a neutral background to complement the owner's colourful objects and furnishings, with the exception of two red columns that frame the large windows of the living area. These windows open up with unexpected depth onto views over the city.

The entrance is deliberately designed as a compressed space that expands as the visitor proceeds toward the living area. A lower false ceiling works as a reference point for the private area, which comprises three bedrooms, three bathrooms, a laundry and walk-in closets.

PHOTOGRAPHY: Paolo Monello

Floor area: 220 square meters / 2368 square feet

Program: Renovation of existing apartment

Ceiling height/s: From 2.5 to 2.8 meters / 8 to 9 feet

Rooms: Living/dining room, kitchen, lounge seating area with library, three bedrooms (one with ensuite), three bathrooms, walk-in closet and laundry area

Ventilation: Low-airspeed ceiling plenum and blow-out zone integrated with wall wash lighting armature hidden from main viewing directions

Sound attenuation: Floor insulation, drywall partitions with acoustic infill, sound- and vibration-insulated mechanical equipment and air-handling unit placed outside to reduce noise

Green features: Glazing with low solar entrée

1 Entrance
2 Kitchen
3 Living
4 Bedroom
5 Bathroom
6 Walk in closet
7 Laundry

Capri Apartment

CAPRI, ITALY M. Campi, L. Giusti (gbc architetti)

Floor area: 175 square metres / 1900 square feet (apartment); 220 square metres / 2400 square feet (terrace)

Program: Renovation of a family villa into a contemporary holiday apartment

Ceiling height/s: 2.8 metres to 3.5 metres / 9 feet to 11 feet

Rooms: Five bedrooms, kitchen, living room with dining area and four bathrooms

Ventilation: Blow-out zone integrated and hidden from all viewing directions

Sound attenuation: Floor insulation with foam mattress (a high-density acoustic insulation that exhibits high resistance to compressive loads, maintaining a lightweight characteristic and reducing noise)

Green features: Natural ventilation favoured by geometry and position of windows

'Pure and contemporary' was the brief provided by two young Neapolitan professionals who wanted to renovate their International style family villa to create a summer shelter and a place for regenerating weekends less than an hour from the city chaos.

The result constitutes a mix of contemporary design and Mediterranean spirit in keeping with the wonderful surrounding island landscape. Indeed, the panorama of Capri seems to enter the apartment and play a role in all of the important spaces.

The barycentre of the house is undoubtedly the great living room, which looks like a platform over the sea. A spectacular glass window frames the vista of the famous Faraglioni stacks and Marina Piccola bay in its entirety. This perspective of the sea constitutes an element of such beauty and fascination that it became the generating point of the entire spatial layout. All rooms participate with and enjoy the constant presence of the sky and the sea.

The metaphor of the sea can also be found in the furniture, much of which is architect-designed. Dynamic geometries—offering surfaces to support the television and other audiovisual equipment—symbolise the bridges of great ships and combined with the large, panoramic windows create the feeling of being in a luxury cabin of a great cruise ship.

PHOTOGRAPHY: Mario Ferrara

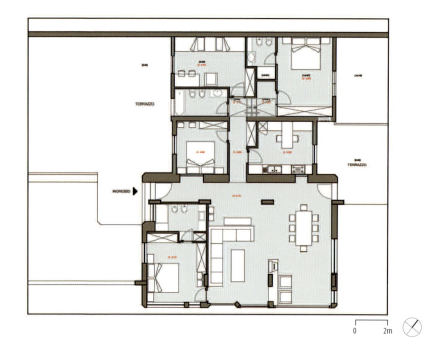

Carr Apartment

SAN FRANCISCO, CALIFORNIA, USA **Craig Steely Architecture**

Floor area: 130 square metres / 1400 square feet

Program: Remodel of a corner apartment in a high-rise building

Ceiling height/s: 2.4 metres / 8 feet

Rooms: Entry foyer; to the left an open living/entertaining/dining room; to the right an open master bedroom/bathroom suite, a guest bathroom and study

Ventilation: The apartment has great cross ventilation precluding the need for air conditioning

Sound attenuation: Acoustically detached ceiling coffers, heavily insulated joining walls and double-glazed windows

Green features: Bonded logic recycled denim insulation, low-E heat resistant glazing, motorised translucent screens on all windows and LED lighting

In this thoroughly modern apartment a floor-to-ceiling ambient light installation offers a striking counterpoint to the city views. The inspiration for the light wall, which runs the length of the east interior wall, was the mood set by 1970s space-rock and ambient music pioneers such as Cluster, Harmonia, Brian Eno and Michael Rother. A computer is programmed with a variety of videos, including sunlight sparkling on Lake Merritt, cows grazing in a field and fish in a tank, among others. The videos are slowed down and each pixel is transmitted to 5-centimetre (2-inch) LEDs behind floor-to-ceiling walls of acid-etched glass, effectively blowing out any sharpness of the video and creating slowly moving ambient light patterns.

The client's simple program gave the architect room to focus on the experience and materials. The apartment is a mixture of reflections and textures, featuring walls, doors and cabinetry of figured Koa and Macassar ebony, brindle brown carpet, thick walls of etched and back-painted glass (some opaque, some translucent) and thick counters of 1-centimetre (3/8-inch) grained stainless steel.

The architect selected all of the furniture as well as the art, emphasising a soothing, calm spatial limbo. Its elevation is so high and the view so picturesque that the apartment sometimes seems removed and unreal, almost two-dimensional. In contrast, the light wall appears three-dimensional—as the LEDs brighten and dim behind the thick etched glass, the wall seems to swell and contract like waves in the ocean or a living, breathing thing.

PHOTOGRAPHY: Rien von Rijthoven

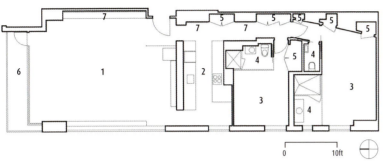

1	Living
2	Kitchen
3	Bedroom
4	Bathroom
5	Storage
6	Deck
7	Light wall

Collector's Loft

GREENWICH VILLAGE, NEW YORK, USA   UNStudio

Credits: Ben van Berkel with Arjan Dingsté, Marianthi Tatari and Colette Parras

Floor area: 550 square metres / 5900 square feet

Program: Renovation of loft into apartment and private gallery

Ceiling height/s: 2.7 metres / 9.5 feet (average) with certain zones arched up around 12 centimetres (5 inches) to create the effect of an indeterminate ceiling height

Rooms: Two bedrooms with ensuites, kitchen, gallery with dining and lounge seating areas, library, coat room and art storage room

Ventilation: Low-airspeed ceiling plenum and blow-out zone integrated with wall wash lighting armature (hidden from main viewing directions)

Sound attenuation: Floor and ceiling insulation, acoustically detached walls, acoustically heavily insulated mechanical equipment (also vibration insulated) and air-handling unit placed outside to reduce noise

Green features: Good insulation, glass with low solar entrée, motor operated translucent screens for all windows and LED lighting

The design of this loft in downtown Manhattan explores the interaction between a gallery and living space. The client, a collector, sought a comfortable living environment in which he could interact with the many paintings, objects and books in his collection. The loft aims to merge life and art by facilitating these daily interactions.

The meandering walls frame an open space that privileges long perspectives, with sheltered corners and niches nestled in the curves. Within this hybrid space exhibition areas merge into the living areas; a floating exhibition wall blends into library shelves on one side and a display case on the other side.

While the walls form a calm and controlled backdrop for the works of art, the ceiling comprises a field of ambient and local lighting conditions, providing an organisational element in the exhibition and living areas. The opaque part of the ceiling consists of subtly arched elements that evoke a limitless ceiling and disguise the real height of the space.

The luminous part of the ceiling is backlit by 18,000 LED lights. This extensive membrane of light serves multiple purposes: it balances the proportions of the loft by creating an illusion of height, functions as unobtrusive space divider, and can be programmed to illuminate the space with various shades of light, from the coolest, most neutral daylight to warmer tones.

The third element essential to this design is an appreciation of the city, which is expressed in the framing of the views. The original windows in the south wall were replaced with floor-to-ceiling panes that frame and extend compelling views of downtown Manhattan.

As a finishing element, Douglas fir flooring with half-metre (1.5-feet) wide planks covers the entire loft. The subtle, even-toned floor unifies the space and allows furniture and art to be positioned as floating elements in changeable constellations.

PHOTOGRAPHY: Iwan Baan

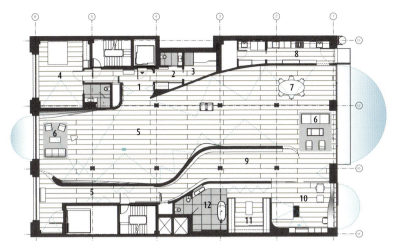

1 Vestibule
2 Coat room
3 Art storage
4 Guest room
5 Exhibition
6 Seating
7 Dining
8 Kitchen
9 Library
10 Bedroom
11 Walk-in closet
12 Bathroom

Fifth Avenue Townhouse

NEW YORK CITY, NEW YORK, UNITED STATES **Mojo Stumer Associates, p.c.**

Floor area: 540 square metres / 5800 square feet

Program: Interior and exterior remodel of a four-storey townhouse apartment

Ceiling height/s: 3.5 metres / 11.5 feet

Rooms: Three bedrooms with full bathroom, chef's kitchen, formal and casual dining, office with glass floor, gym, movie theatre, entry foyer on a separate lower level, bar and two outdoor patios

The complete interior and exterior renovation of this four-storey, five-bedroom private townhouse located in the coveted upper east side of Manhattan took close to two years to complete.

The discerning owners were intrigued by the concept of starting with a clean slate. The goal was to design a living space that would complement their lifestyle as well as their taste for luxury. A streamlined, hard-edged study of material and movement, combined with an inviting and engaging floor plan, became the intent.

The apartment features a state-of-the-art gym, a private office with a glass floor revealing the custom mahogany kitchen below, multiple private outdoor decks and a spectacular spiral staircase with a hand-cast iron banister and massive crystal chandelier. The home also serves as a showcase for the owner's extensive and vibrant art collection.

An eclectic mix of contemporary and antique furnishings rests on a canvas of statuary marble that would make Bernini envious. Exploiting the access to natural light was also important. The polished finishes become beacons of refracted light and work together with the neutral colour palette to create a soft, ambient glow throughout the entire space.

PHOTOGRAPHY: Mark D. Stumer

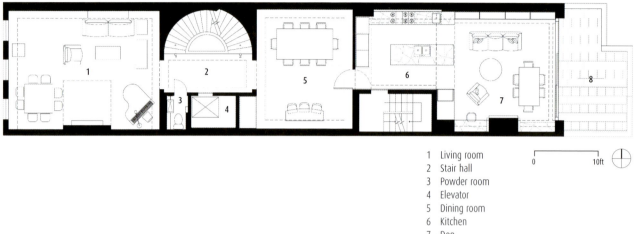

1 Living room
2 Stair hall
3 Powder room
4 Elevator
5 Dining room
6 Kitchen
7 Den
8 Outdoor deck

FILC Apartment

MESTRE, ITALY **Filippo Caprioglio – Caprioglio Associati Studio di Architettura**

The concepts behind this design are simple yet essential. The key idea was to enhance the perception of depth and height within the apartment by exposing the system of sectional and longitudinal circulation.

The apartment was completely reorganised according to the needs and living habits of a family of four, including two young children. A spacious living area is organised around the couch, which forms a centrally located island. This layout is influenced by a series of windows on two sides of the room and the monolithic stone fireplace on another. A special paint used on the upper part of the chimney allows it to be used as a cinema projection screen, thus precluding the need to accommodate a television.

The kitchen is located inside a self-contained freestanding cube that sits apart from the original wooden structure of the roof. The top of the cube also provides alignment for the glass surface that marks the entrance and separates it from the main access stair. This area provides a threshold zone for the private area of the apartment where the bedroom, the children's playroom and bathrooms are located. The third bedroom, which also functions as a studio, is accessible from the living space. Placed in sequence with main living room, the large terrace guarantees access to natural light and opens up the entire space.

PHOTOGRAPHY: Paolo Belvedere

Floor area: 130 square metres / 1400 square feet
Program: New apartment for a family of four
Ceiling height/s: 2.7 meters to 3.5 metres / 9 feet to 11.5 feet
Rooms: Living/dining room, terrace, kitchen, library/office, three bedrooms (one with ensuite) and two bathrooms
Ventilation: Air-conditioning split system
Sound attenuation: Floor insulation and air-handling unit placed outside to reduce noise

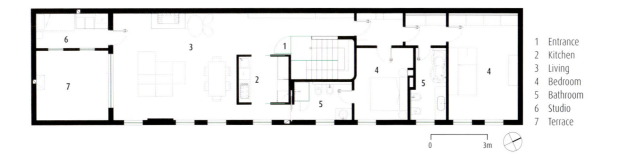

1 Entrance
2 Kitchen
3 Living
4 Bedroom
5 Bathroom
6 Studio
7 Terrace

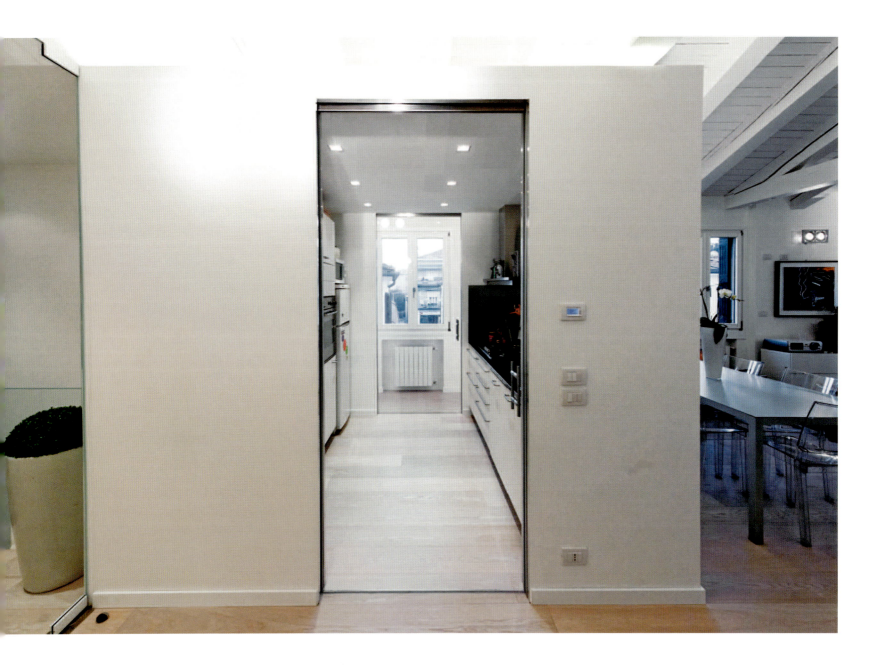

Harbour's Edge

AUCKLAND, NEW ZEALAND   **Hulena Architects Ltd**

Floor area: 160 square metres / 1700 square feet

Program: New loft apartment contained within an upper floor of a refurbished early 20th-century commercial building on the waterfront of Auckland City

Ceiling height/s: 4 metres / 13 feet

Rooms: Entry foyer, great room with living/dining/kitchen, library, two mezzanine bedrooms, two bathrooms, dressing room and wine cellar

Ventilation: The location of the apartment at the corner of the building affords good cross ventilation and the bathrooms and kitchen are vented to the roof

Sound attenuation: New wide-board solid timber overlay flooring is spaced off the existing concrete structure on timber battens bedded on compressed rubber sound insulation and interior walls are double stud, acoustically detached, sound insulated and sound rated

Green features: The apartment faces north and west catching all day sun and the internal thermal mass of the building stores heat for re-radiation overnight; windows are clad with operable bi-fold timber shutters, which offer a multitude of options for controlling sunlight penetration during the day and at night the shutters can be closed down to contain the stored heat as necessary

This apartment is located in a stately heritage-listed building on a prominent corner fronting Auckland's Waitemata Harbour. The key feature of this building, which was constructed of reinforced concrete and founded on kauri piles circa 1915, is the large central light well that runs the height of the building and enables natural light to penetrate down into the original commercial floors. The space was purchased as a shell for its location on the northern corner of the building, which overlooks the harbour and Auckland's main street and affords daylong sunlight.

The apartment was designed as a city retreat with space to accommodate guests. The concept was to amplify a diagonal entry to the apartment and capture views of the Ferry Building—which sits on the harbour's edge beyond—and also to maximise the 4-metre stud height around the perimeter of the space.

The welcoming entry is framed by stairs, which provide separate access to the two mezzanine-level bedroom spaces. The two bathrooms are sheathed in aluminium-composite cladding, which hides storage spaces. The centrally located kitchen provides a focal point for entertaining and the various living spaces revolve around it. Within the dining space, concealed storage and display shelves run full height. The library, tucked under the second bedroom with concealed storage and display shelves, overlooks the harbour.

The shell was replastered in white, with wide-board jarrah timber flooring anchoring the space. All internal partitioned walls and built-in joinery are clad with nautically inspired, vertically grooved linings. The full-height doors close on hinges to reduce the need for handles and the majority of the built-in cabinetry has touch latches.

The raised landing defines the entry space and also accommodates plumbing between the bathroom and kitchen areas. The overlay timber floor allows electrical wiring for power, light, sound and technology to be circulated throughout without the need to follow the concrete structure. Plumbing for the fire sprinklers was drilled through the concrete beam structure to raise it above the sight lines. The result is a sophisticated urban living environment.

PHOTOGRAPHY: Kallan MacLeod

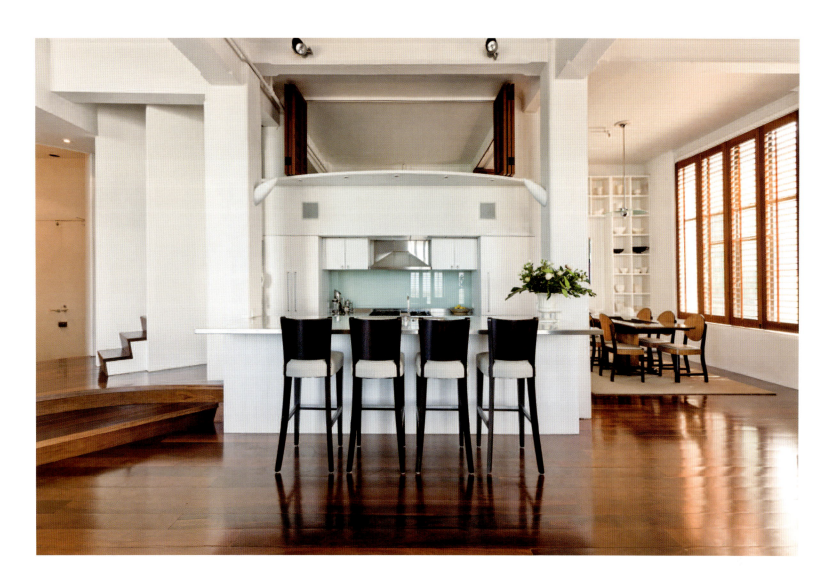

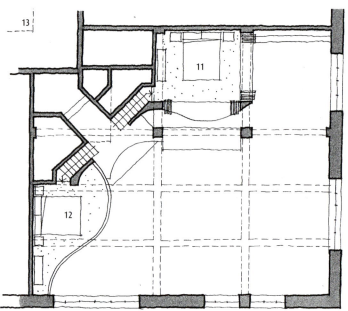

Mezzanine floor plan

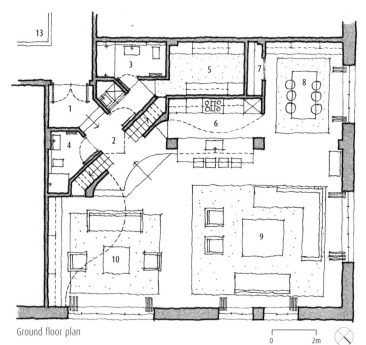

Ground floor plan 0 2m

1	Entry	8	Dining
2	Raised landing	9	Living
3	Bathroom one	10	Library
4	Bathroom two	11	Bedroom one
5	Dressing room	12	Bedroom two
6	Kitchen	13	Light well
7	Wine storage		

Highpoint

HIGHGATE, LONDON, UNITED KINGDOM **Adam Richards Architects**

Floor area: 100 square metres / 1100 square feet

Program: Refurbishment of a large flat in a heritage-listed building

Ceiling height/s: 2.6 metres / 8.5 feet

Rooms: Three bedrooms, one bathroom, one powder room, living/dining room, kitchen, study, hallway and balcony

Ventilation: Naturally ventilated

Sound attenuation: Floors are all cork, replicating the original 1935 design

Green features: The building was constructed in the 1930s as 'minimal dwellings'—it was highly efficient at the time and, by keeping it in use, its resources are further conserved

This remodel of one of Berthold Lubetkin's seminal modernist 1933–35 Highpoint flats in Highgate necessitated delicate negotiations with English Heritage. Twentieth-century additions and alterations were removed or reversed, the old kitchen was converted into a study, and the dining room was opened out to become a large family kitchen. New built-in elements in the kitchen, bathroom and study were articulated as freestanding objects in a range of colours—from subtle khaki to flaming fuchsia. A new bookcase, based on an oblique section cut through the building, forms the centrepiece of the flat. It is a 1:10 scale model of a building, within a building.

The interventions emerged from the clients' need for a contemporary family home, as well as the collision between the building's functionalist 'machine aesthetic' and its Grade 1 heritage protection. The bookcase reverses the modernist translation of a filing cabinet as housing and references the Highpoint building's current status as a fetish object. Constructed from timber and steel, it is spray-finished to emulate the building's Corbusian whiteness.

PHOTOGRAPHY: Morley von Sternberg

Humelegården Apartment

STOCKHOLM, SWEDEN

Tham & Videgård Arkitekter / Martin Videgård and Bolle Tham

Credits: Tove Belfrage, Helene Amundsen, Johan Björkholm, Karolina Nyström (collaborators)

Floor area: 375 square metres / 4030 square feet

Program: Refurbishment of an apartment for a family of four, plus a guest studio for visiting relatives and friends

Ceiling height/s: 3.25 metres / 10 feet

Rooms: Ten rooms and a kitchen

Ventilation: Fresh air from window vents and exhaust from bathrooms and kitchen

Sound attenuation: Floor and ceiling insulation

The brief for this residence was to re-establish the well-crafted qualities of a once-elegant turn-of-the-century apartment that had been altered completely and for some time transformed into a hotel, leaving very few traces of the original Art Nouveau design and detailing.

The architects' inspiration came in part from the apartment's location and its plan, which includes a long row of rooms with views of the park outside. Equally important was the idea of experimenting with the traditionally Swedish use of colour and patterns in interiors, which has been developed by artists and architects such as Carl Larsson and Josef Frank.

The overlapping colours transform the layout of the apartment, adding a new structure of spaces that link with each other across the original plan. The oversized and multicoloured natural ash parquet floor offers countless design possibilities. Once the colour set was established, a design for each room was developed in relation to the others. Every piece of parquet was designed to fit into the right position so there were no random factors in the construction process.

The leaded windows were preserved in order to maintain the protected exterior façade and white custom furniture was introduced to further enhance the interiors and create a coherent ensemble.

PHOTOGRAPHY: Åke E:son Lindman

Kent Street Apartment

SYDNEY, NEW SOUTH WALES, AUSTRALIA **RLD**

Credits: Andrea D'Cruz (director) and Louise Spicer (designer)

Floor area: 250 square metres / 2700 square feet

Program: Conversion of an existing apartment with an Art Deco influence into an elegant, contemporary residential space

Ceiling height/s: 2.7 metres / 9 feet

Rooms: Two bedrooms (one with ensuite), study/third bedroom, formal entry foyer, formal living and dining, family room and two balconies

Green features: Re-use of existing furnishings, use of local manufacturers and suppliers, and sustainable materials

Working within the parameters of a distinct period style can present the risk of monotonous replication. For the designer of this apartment interior, it was important that the existing Art Deco style was treated as an essence to which fresh ideas and contemporary elements could be added. Elegance, glamour, function and modernity are at the forefront of this design, remaining true to the Art Deco style.

Formal areas, such as the living and dining room, were adorned in luxurious materials. Silks, mohair, polished and aged metals, waxed leather, hides, imported European natural stone and highly polished timbers were used to reinforce the formality of these spaces. A variety of linens—selected for their relaxed, tactile qualities—feature in casual areas such as the family room and study.

Environmentally sustainable design principles played a large role in the decision to re-use existing furniture—in particular the beds, living room sofas, dining room chairs and study sofas. Furthermore, the use of local manufacturers and suppliers assisted with a reduction in the embodied energy of materials. Sustainable window furnishings were chosen to counter the effects of direct exposure to eastern and western sunlight.

Tonal variations within the monochromatic palette maintain visual interest. Materials of various textures—from polished to highly tactile surfaces—were chosen for their aesthetic appeal as well as their reflective qualities.

PHOTOGRAPHY: Tom Evangelidis

LC Apartment

CUNEO, PIEMONTE, ITALY **Damilanostudio Architects**

This apartment in a new building in the centre of Cuneo was designed for a young building contractor. Taxos Greek marble flooring floods the apartment with white—the protagonist of this design. Polished onsite, the marble tiles create a uniform surface that mirrors a minimal selection of custom-designed furniture pieces. Doussiè wood offers an element of warmth to the atmosphere; it envelopes the dining area and provides a filter between the kitchen and the living area. A wooden platform creates a connection to the original design of the building. The wood, used as cladding in vertical slats, then flows into the bedroom.

The guest bedroom, or study, opens with frosted glass onto a corner of the living room. The main corridor also includes a walk-in closet common to all three bedrooms. The use of recessed lighting contributes to the minimalist environment of the apartment. Only a single reading lamp pendant floats above the chaise longue. The terraces, with teak flooring and large flowerpots, are a green reflection of the view of the mountain ranges and landscape of Cuneo that can be enjoyed from the apartment.

PHOTOGRAPHY: Andrea Martiradonna

Floor area: 150 square metres / 1600 square feet (apartment); 75 square metres / 800 square feet (terrace)

Program: New attic apartment

Ceiling height/s: 2.7 metres / 9 feet

Rooms: Two bedrooms, two bathrooms, living, study, kitchen with storeroom and dining room

Ventilation: Natural ventilation directly integrated with mechanical ventilation system

Sound attenuation: Walls are two sheets of plasterboard with a mineral wool panel interposed, the air-handling unit is placed under the roof to reduce noise and the floor is insulated from impact noise by horizontal dividers

Green features: Triple glazing with low-E coating and argon gas

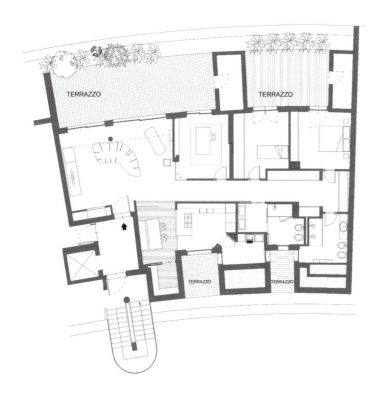

Ludwig Penthouse

SAN FRANCISCO, CALIFORNIA, USA **Craig Steely Architecture**

Floor area: 185 square metres / 2000 square feet

Program: Remodel of a penthouse to create more living space

Ceiling height/s: 2.7 metres / 9 feet

Rooms: Two bedrooms, two bathrooms, a kitchen and a living/entertaining room opening to deck

Ventilation: Cross ventilation precludes the need for air conditioning

Sound attenuation: Acoustically detached ceiling coffers, heavily insulated joining walls and double-glazed windows

Green features: Bonded Logic recycled denim insulation, low-E heat-resistant glazing, motorised translucent screens on all windows and LED lighting

The original four-bedroom/four-bathroom plan of this penthouse—located atop a concrete high-rise building overlooking San Francisco's Aquatic Park—was a confusing rabbit warren of rooms. Its numerous partitions diminished the potential vastness of the views of the Golden Gate to the Bay Bridge to the north, and of the city looking south, and also created rooms that were unbearably hot on the south side and freezing cold on the north.

The architect's solution opens up the volume where uses flow together and allows the apartment to naturally temper itself—with natural cross ventilation providing cooling and sunlight providing passive heating. In the previous plan the rooms were positioned on an east/west axis, with a central hall in the middle. The new design switched the orientation of the few walls that were reinstated to north/south, so the bay and city views are seen simultaneously from almost any position in the apartment. Another dimension discovered after the existing walls were demolished was that the gentle arc of the high-rise's plan could be accentuated in the apartment (the building radiates from a point 330 feet to the south). Aluminium strips were inlaid in the dark ipe floor and continuous black light trays were installed in the ceiling along the building's radius.

The elevator delivers the visitor into the apartment's foyer, where a floor-to-ceiling mosaic wall of hand-cut glass covers the north wall. To the east is the public space and to the west is the private area—a study on the south and the master bedroom/bathroom and steam room to the north. A floating mirrored divider and walls of acid-etched glass of varying opacity create privacy.

The architect addressed environmental responsibility by tempering the space as naturally as possible with passive cooling and heating. In addition, Bonded Logic recycled denim insulation and soundproofing was utilised. All the cabinetry veneers and wooden slabs are from the same black walnut tree, which blew down near Napa seven years ago. The design team were lucky to find the local cabinetmaker who had been storing these beautiful slabs, waiting for a job where all could be used together.

PHOTOGRAPHY: Rien von Rijthoven

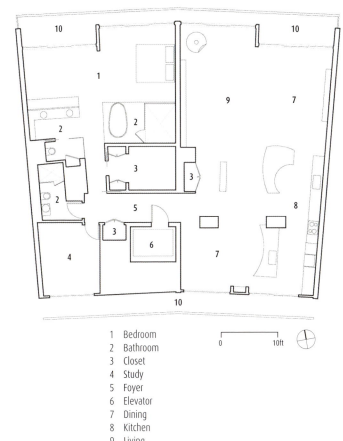

1 Bedroom
2 Bathroom
3 Closet
4 Study
5 Foyer
6 Elevator
7 Dining
8 Kitchen
9 Living
10 Terrace

Manhattan Apartment

NEW YORK CITY, NEW YORK, USA **Mojo Stumer Associates, p.c.**

Floor area: 575 square metres / 6200 square feet

Program: Remodeled apartment over four floors incorporating an extensive art collection

Ceiling height/s: 3.6 metres / 12 feet

Rooms: Two bedrooms with full bathrooms, kosher chef's kitchen, formal living space, family room, powder room, library, casual and formal dining, elevator foyer, gallery, office and gym

The owners of this apartment wanted a space that incorporated their extensive and world-renowned art collection with modern architecture and traditional decorating. This balance is evident throughout, as the clean lines of the built environment work perfectly in juxtaposition with the stout, asymmetrical characteristics of the furnishings and accessories.

Linear cast-bronze archways act as portholes between the different areas of the apartment, framing perfectly proportionate spaces. Tray ceilings in high-gloss lacquer and Bianco Dolomiti flooring accentuate and reflect the light from the massive crystal chandeliers in the entry foyer.

The kitchen is state of the art with rift-cut white oak millwork featuring a serrated finish and white Glassos countertop and floor tiles. The dining room features walls upholstered in velvet and crystal beaded wallpaper set in to the tray ceiling above the three custom-designed crystal chandeliers. Back- and up-lit glass and bronze display cabinetry was custom designed for the clients' massive Steuben glass collection and all of the door hardware in the apartment is cast bronze to match the accents throughout.

PHOTOGRAPHY: Paul Warchol

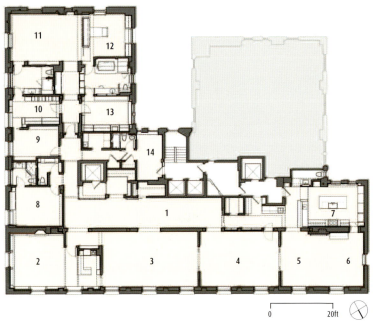

1 Gallery
2 Library
3 Living room
4 Dining room
5 Family room
6 Breakfast area
7 Kitchen
8 Guest bedroom
9 Gym
10 His closet
11 Master bedroom
12 Her study
13 Her closet
14 Maid's bedroom

The Mansion on Peachtree

ATLANTA, GEORGIA, USA **Harrison Design Associates**

Floor area: 340 square metres / 3700 square feet

Program: New condominium in a high-rise apartment building

Ceiling height/s: From 2.75 metres to 4.75 metres / 9 feet to 15 feet

Rooms: Two bedrooms, two-and-a-half bathrooms, open-plan living/dining/kitchen, TV lounge, study, laundry and terrace

Ventilation: HVAC—water-source heat pumps tied to base building chilled water loop with ducted supply and plenum return (all supply and return registers are trimless slot diffusers for a clean, uncluttered look)

Sound attenuation: An additional wall placed in front of the apartment's demising walls, an acoustical cork layer placed between the concrete slab and wood flooring subfloor, elevated walls in mechanical room with sound-attenuating insulation, heat pumps on vibration isolators and sound-attenuating insulation placed in master bedroom and common hallway walls

Green features: Reclaimed teak from demolished pole buildings in Thailand, low- and no-VOC materials, high-efficiency mechanical systems, dual-flush toilets, water conserving showerheads and high-efficiency LED cove lighting

Contrasting with Robert A.M. Stern's classic New York-style residential tower, this condominium at The Mansion on Peachtree exemplifies a decidedly modern approach to spatial organisation and use of materials. It addresses specific client-driven needs both spatially and programmatically while exploring architectonic ideas of shape and texture.

An angled wall of plaster, steel and wood with an exposed structural column pulls the visitor in, becoming a singular element that defines the openness of the main living spaces, while at the same time concealing support functions. This aggressive angularity is softened by a whimsical egg-shaped column that stands freely at the implied intersection of these spaces.

From a 1200-pound custom-engineered steel door that effortlessly pivots to access the study, to a handmade metal rolling ladder providing artful access to kitchen storage and a steel-clad fireplace wall that conceals a puzzle box of hidden cabinets, customised design elements enhance the ambiance, indulge an interest and turn routine organisation into an art form. Fully integrated audio, visual, lighting and shading systems modulate the flow of light and sound with push-button precision.

PHOTOGRAPHY: Sarah Dorio

1 Entry vestibule
2 Laundry
3 Bathroom
4 Closet
5 Master bedroom
6 Guest suite
7 Study
8 Living
9 Terrace
10 TV lounge
11 Dining
12 Kitchen

Maria Borges Apartment

LISBON, PORTUGAL   **Atelier Bugio Arquitectura**

Credits: João Favila Menezes (principal architect)

Floor area: 175 square metres / 1900 square feet

Program: Conversion of the top floor and attic in a historic building into a modern apartment

Ceiling height/s: 2.6 metres / 8.5 feet

The brief for this project was to convert the top floor and attic of an 18th-century Pombaline building into a contemporary apartment without sacrificing its historical characteristics. The redesign allows light, layout and materials to influence the space and highlight the living experience over the two floors.

The lower floor comprises the social area where the extant structure and materials were restored and natural light penetrates through mansard windows. The top floor has an open loft structure. Ridge vents reflect light on the white lacquered floor, making the space brighter. In contrast, the lower floor has bare wooden flooring and the lath walls and wood ceilings are painted white.

The two floors have clearly distinct functions. The lower floor has two adjoining reception rooms with small recesses for reading, working and multimedia. The north-facing kitchen, a space for both cooking and eating, is connected to all the service areas, including the utility room and larder/pantry.

The top floor is a single space delimited by two large cupboards. Storage space is contained within the recesses in the roof. Next to the two side gables, two areas defined by the angles of the ridge vent house the shower and toilet.

PHOTOGRAPHY: Leonardo Finotti, 2011 © photo@leonardofinotti.com

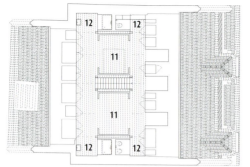

Upper floor plan

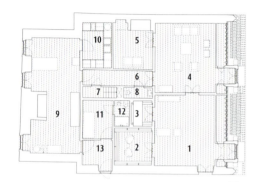

Lower floor plan

0 5m

1 Living
2 Library
3 Study
4 Living
5 TV lounge
6 Hall
7 Stairs
8 Powder room
9 Kitchen/Dining
10 Den
11 Bedroom
12 Bathroom
13 Entry

Melbourne Apartment

MELBOURNE, VICTORIA, AUSTRALIA **fmd architects**

Floor area: 160 square metres / 1720 square feet

Program: Renovation of existing apartment

Ceiling height/s: 2.6 metres / 8.5 feet

Rooms: Three bedrooms, kitchen, living, dining and separate laundry

Ventilation: Ducted air-conditioning system

Sound attenuation: Acoustic insulation to walls and ceilings

Located in a high-rise building within Melbourne's central business district, this apartment enjoys 180-degree views of the city and the bay. The brief was to renovate the existing kitchen and laundry and complete a general upgrade of the finishes, fittings and lighting. The main bedroom was improved to provide a place of retreat for the owners and the entry to the ensuite was concealed within the robes, while the remaining two bedrooms were adapted to serve dual functions as studies.

The clients had spent the past decade living in the Middle East and during this time accumulated an extensive collection of furniture, objects and artworks, which needed to be considered in the design process. Rich, dark tones were selected for the joinery and flooring to complement the heavily detailed bronze items, Persian rugs and a copper-detailed dining table. These dark tones enhance the experience of the city views, while the white walls reflect the natural light penetrating the space and offer a neutral background for the rich colours of the artworks.

The material and colour selection in the kitchen reinforces the rich palette, with bronzed stainless steel cupboards and warm greys alongside the dark timber veneers. Royal blue was introduced into feature recess pulls on the dining side of the joinery, referencing the Persian rugs. In contrast, a lighter palette was used for the bedrooms to expand the sense of space within them.

The resulting design offers a rich and varied palette that reflects the particularities of the clients and provides a strong connection to the surrounding landscape and views.

PHOTOGRAPHY: Tanja Milbourne

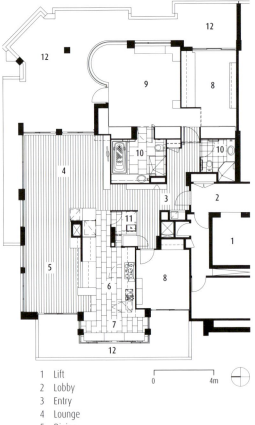

1. Lift
2. Lobby
3. Entry
4. Lounge
5. Dining
6. Kitchen
7. Meals
8. Bedroom
9. Master bedroom
10. Bathroom
11. Laundry
12. Balcony

Milsons Point

MILSONS POINT, NEW SOUTH WALES, AUSTRALIA **Stanic Harding**

Floor area: 150 square metres / 1600 square feet

Program: Complete stripping out and redesign of an existing three-bedroom apartment on the ninth floor of a high-rise apartment building

Ceiling height/s: 2.5 metres / 8 feet

Rooms: Master bedroom with ensuite and dressing room, second bedroom, bathroom/laundry, study, open kitchen and living/dining areas, enclosed and open balconies

Ventilation: An energy-efficient air-conditioning system replaced the old system, multilayered black-out and block-out retractable blinds, cross ventilation achieved through enclosing existing balcony and using full-height banks of operable louvres

Sound attenuation: Acoustically rated timber flooring

Green features: Windows were treated with colour-corrected film, cutting out 65 percent of potential heat gain

The brief for this project was to create a beautiful space that would encourage the owners away from their South Coast retreat and back into the city. A particular stipulation was that the rarely used, southwest-facing, triangular balcony be enclosed.

Prior to its renovation the apartment was uninteresting and poorly planned. The existing layout presented a low internal central corridor and a land-locked entry. Enclosed rooms ran along the perimeter of the building, denying the occupants a connection to views and light, with the corridor space only opening at the living room.

The architect's approach was to open up the apartment by fusing circulation spaces with habitable spaces. The planning rationale allowed all major spaces to connect to the edge of the building and the wonderful views of the harbour, Luna Park and Walsh Bay. Incorporating the existing external balcony and corridor space into the apartment allowed for planning options that were not possible previously. The balcony now operates as a dining space, with the added benefits of an outdoor space. It also links the main bedroom to the apartment in a way that reinforces the main bedroom's seclusion from the general living areas.

The design seeks to balance the connection to the extensive views and the focus on internal spaces. Joinery is used as a second layer in the scheme to create elements of interest that sometimes frame views and sometimes become the focus. These space-making elements are carefully detailed and connected; some are highly reflective and rich while others are plain and white. Colour is used on walls and joinery furthest from the edge elements, which are white. Joinery wall panelling conceals services, storage, laundry and bathroom areas from the casual visitor. The use of mirrors on walls and doors also extends space and brings in the harbour views. The kitchen plays a central role as both a space maker and a viewing platform, with the latter function reinforced by a change in floor level.

PHOTOGRAPHY: Paul Gosney

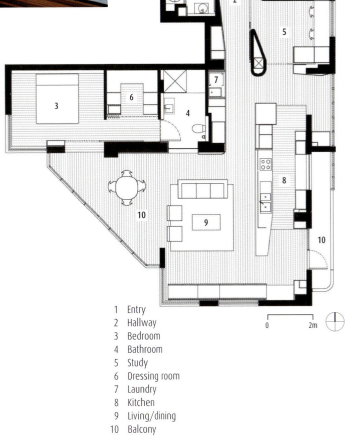

1 Entry
2 Hallway
3 Bedroom
4 Bathroom
5 Study
6 Dressing room
7 Laundry
8 Kitchen
9 Living/dining
10 Balcony

Mini Loft

LJUBLJANA, SLOVENIA **OFIS Arhitekti**

The brief for this apartment was to organise a functional living space within a very small shell for a single male client. The most important task was to maximise the living area, which is complemented by service spaces including an entrance, kitchenette, workspace, bathroom, bedroom and audio and visual areas—all within 30 square metres. The dimensions of the service spaces were deliberately kept to a minimum. They are displaced around the main room, forming a sort of enclosed cupboard.

The sliding doors providing access to the service areas form a striking design feature. Made of semi-transparent Perspex (polymethil metacrilate), they are printed with a blurred image of trees. During the daytime this envelope appears to be an opaque, solid wall. At night the envelope becomes a bright light box, creating an atmosphere similar to nocturnal city lights.

PHOTOGRAPHY: Tomaz Gregoric

Credits: Rok Oman, Spela Videcnik

Floor area: 30 square metres / 320 square feet

Program: Renovation of a tiny loft into a functional living space for one person

Ceiling height/s: 2.75 metres / 9 feet

Rooms: Central living space, bedroom box, kitchen box and bathroom box

Ventilation: Natural ventilation via double windows

Sound attenuation: Floor and ceiling insulation and acoustically detached walls

Green features: Good insulation, double window doors and LED lighting

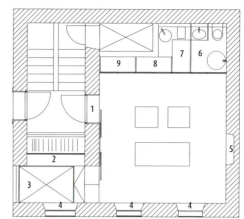

1	Entry box
2	Dressing box
3	Bed box
4	Light box
5	CD box
6	Toilet box
7	Cook box
8	TV box
9	Communications box

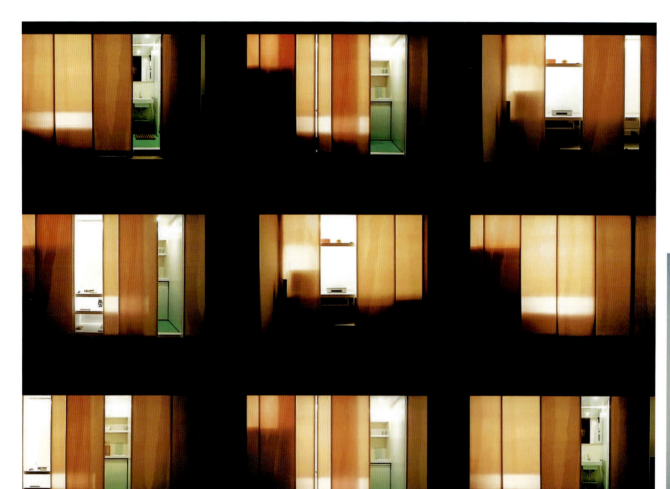

New York Apartment

NEW YORK CITY, NEW YORK, USA **Zivkovic Connolly Architects**

Credits: Bridget Nisivoccia (interior decorator), Charles G Michel (systems engineering) and Windsor A.R (general contractor)

Floor area: 380 square metres / 4100 square feet (apartment); 140 square metres / 1500 square feet (terrace)

Program: Penthouse duplex apartment

Ceiling height/s: Ranging from 6.5 metres (atrium) to 2.5 metres (mezzanine) / 21.5 feet (atrium) to 8 feet (mezzanine)

Rooms: Living, dining, kitchen and family rooms, a master bedroom suite, two children's bedrooms with a shared bathroom, a home theatre, a powder room and separate home office areas for both the husband and wife

Ventilation: Multi-zone ducted central air-conditioning system and separate exhaust systems for bathrooms and kitchen

Sound attenuation: Air-conditioning system compressors are located at roof level, insulated double-glazing mitigates street noise and interior walls are filled with fibreglass sound-attenuating insulation

Green features: Enhanced day-lighting, non-VOC paint and sealing finishes, water-efficient plumbing fixtures, energy star appliances and insulated glazing treated with low-E film

This penthouse duplex apartment is situated in a former industrial loft building that was converted for residential use. The program required a significant number of cellular rooms and the floor area to be split over two levels. The design exploits height and volume rather than floor area alone to achieve a generous and expansive feeling.

The bedrooms are located around the perimeter, with access to daylight and natural ventilation. Accessory spaces, including the laundry, home theatre and various bathrooms, occupy the innermost areas that lack access to windows. Maintaining an open, loft-like feel, the living room is a dramatic, double-height, centrally located atrium that receives daylight from two levels.

Surrounding this central hub, but partially screened from it, the circulation routes are defined by long, uninterrupted expanses of wall that enhance the sense of scale. The connecting interior stair is positioned directly below an elongated skylight and is thus, like the major spaces, washed in natural light. Upstairs, at the mezzanine level, the kitchen is situated near a matching elongated skylight facing the family room and the roof terrace beyond. At this level, the dining and family rooms were arranged to be open to each other and to overlook the living room below. A continuous wall of glazed, south-facing doors gives access to a private roof terrace, adding to the expansiveness of the upper floor.

In keeping with the client's request for a bright, sunlit interior, the dominant background colour tends toward a creamy white. Concentrated expanses of bolder colours executed in polished Venetian plaster provide accents within the main areas. A continuous wall of cherry panelling conceals the doors to the powder room, home theatre and other secondary spaces. Natural flooring materials, including a light-coloured Italian stone and wide plank Brazilian mahogany, give warmth, variety and texture to the overall palette. Brushed stainless steel railings and matching door hardware introduce an element of fine detail, which contrasts with the broader surfaces.

PHOTOGRAPHY: Andrea Brizzi and Ty Cole

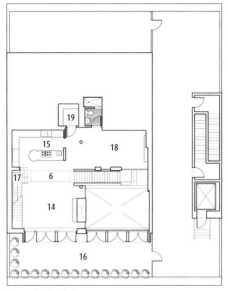
Mezzanine level plan

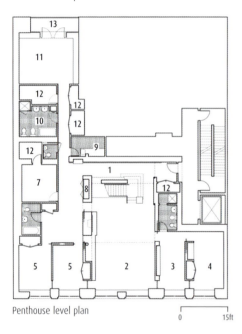
Penthouse level plan

0   15ft

1 Gallery
2 Living room
3 Her office
4 His office
5 Bedroom
6 Skylight (above)
7 Media room
8 Wet bar
9 Laundry/linen
10 Master bathroom
11 Master bedroom
12 Closet/storage
13 Terrace
14 Family room
15 Kitchen
16 Lower terrace
17 Stairs to upper roof
18 Dining
19 Pantry

Norman Reach Penthouse

NORMAN REACH, QUEENSLAND, AUSTRALIA **RLD**

Credits: Andrea D'Cruz (director), Billy Fleming (designer) and Lisa Trani (designer)

Floor area: 330 square metres / 3500 square feet (apartment); 170 square metres / 1800 square feet (balconies)

Program: New penthouse apartment

Ceiling height/s: Ranging from 2.4 to 5 metres / 8 to 16 feet

Rooms: Formal entry, living/dining, family room, kitchen, four bedrooms, study, one bathroom, two ensuites and a powder room, four balconies

Ventilation: Fan-assisted natural ventilation and mechanical ventilation options

Sound attenuation: Acoustic floor underlay and solid walls

Green features: Northerly aspect with deep balcony overhangs for summer sun deflection

The beauty of this penthouse is in the generosity of its spatial volumes. The contemporary interior design language maintains a 'less is more' approach.

Embracing intentionally understated ideals, the client's admiration of the simplicity and modesty of 1950s style formed the design platform. The apartment features original pieces of furniture from this era along with a selection of contemporary pieces that were added to the mix in recognition of the modern architectural context.

Spaces such as the formal living/dining area, the kitchen/family room and two outdoor terraces all interconnect seamlessly. As each space is visible from the other, a congruent design language was applied, while subtle variances maintain interest throughout.

The predominantly cool palette is juxtaposed with the sub-tropical Brisbane climate. Driven by the natural plywood finish of the formal living room ceiling and an instinctive human desire for warmth, the designer chose natural and neutral tones to form a balance within the cool palette. Materials such as leather, hide, wool, timber and stone feature dominantly—in line with the client's appreciation of traditional materials.

PHOTOGRAPHY: Tom Evangelidis

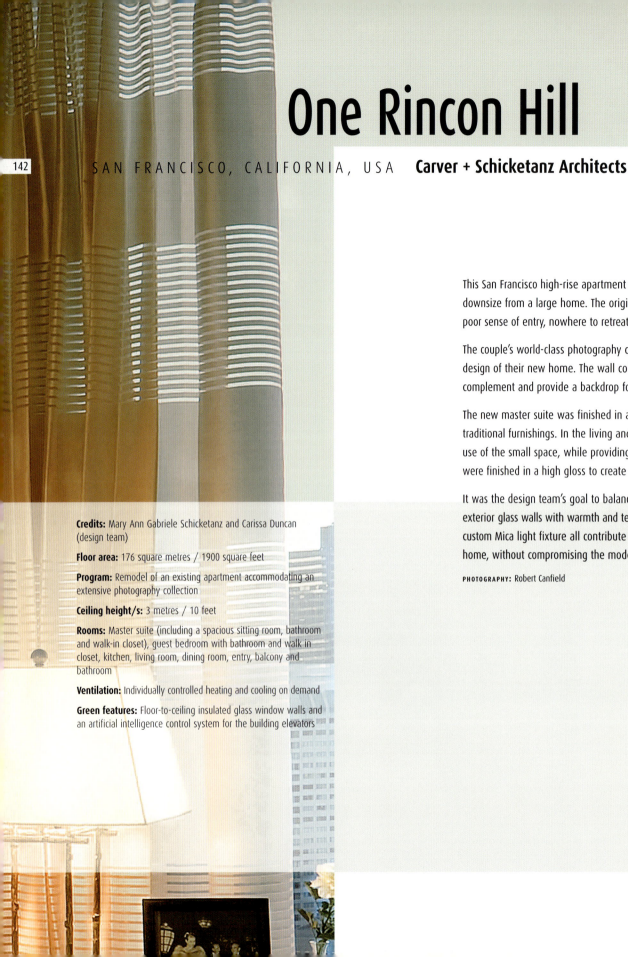

One Rincon Hill

SAN FRANCISCO, CALIFORNIA, USA **Carver + Schicketanz Architects**

This San Francisco high-rise apartment was designed for a retired couple who wished to downsize from a large home. The original three-bedroom, two-bathroom layout had a poor sense of entry, nowhere to retreat to, small bedrooms and several narrow hallways.

The couple's world-class photography collection became the inspiration for the interior design of their new home. The wall colour and fabric palette were chosen to both complement and provide a backdrop for the art.

The new master suite was finished in a romantic style, with pastel lacquers and traditional furnishings. In the living and dining room, a built-in banquette makes best use of the small space, while providing the ability to host up to 12 guests. The ceilings were finished in a high gloss to create the illusion of additional height.

It was the design team's goal to balance the stark architecture of floor-to-ceiling exterior glass walls with warmth and texture. Silk and wool rugs, rich woods and a large custom Mica light fixture all contribute to the sense of comfort in the client's new home, without compromising the modern architecture.

PHOTOGRAPHY: Robert Canfield

Credits: Mary Ann Gabriele Schicketanz and Carissa Duncan (design team)

Floor area: 176 square metres / 1900 square feet

Program: Remodel of an existing apartment accommodating an extensive photography collection

Ceiling height/s: 3 metres / 10 feet

Rooms: Master suite (including a spacious sitting room, bathroom and walk-in closet), guest bedroom with bathroom and walk in closet, kitchen, living room, dining room, entry, balcony and bathroom

Ventilation: Individually controlled heating and cooling on demand

Green features: Floor-to-ceiling insulated glass window walls and an artificial intelligence control system for the building elevators

1 Entry
2 Kitchen
3 Dining room
4 Living room
5 Master sitting
6 Master bedroom
7 Master bathroom
8 Bathroom
9 Guest bedroom

Organic Space

WUXI, CHINA **MoHen Design International**

Built with comparatively organic materials and a simple structure, this apartment allows the resident to enjoy natural lighting and the sounds of nature in a pure and healthy living environment.

The first floor is separated into two main areas: one half is the living room and the other the bedroom. The design ensures that there are no obstacles within the public area and utilises the full extent of the space.

The stair to the basement is contained within an open storage area with a semi-transparent skin—the stairs are barely visible behind it. A wall closet in the master bedroom also utilises glass to separate the living room and master bedroom while allowing some visual penetrability. The open-plan master bedroom suite comprises the sleeping area with a bathroom, study and dressing area.

Task lights hidden in the top of the closet can also be used as lighting for the living room. An opening in the lower side of the television wall in the living room connects with the study area in the master bedroom allowing a visual 'break'.

The primary function of the basement is to provide a relaxing area to enjoy the sauna and spa while offering space for drinking tea, practising yoga and reading. Every inch of this area connects with the view outside. The tea area within and the artificial waterfall outside combine beautifully, creating a strong yet still impact. A light well in the basement ceiling above the oversized bathtub allows sunlight to rain down on the bather.

PHOTOGRAPHY: MoHen Design International/Maoder Chou

Floor area: 200 square metres / 2100 square feet
Program: New apartment incorporating a spa area with space for traditional tea ceremonies and practising yoga
Ceiling height/s: 3 metres / 10 feet
Rooms: Dining room, lounge seating areas, coatroom, study, master bedroom and bathroom, basement
Ventilation: Central air-conditioning equipment and central dust removal system
Sound attenuation: Floor and ceiling insulation
Green features: LED lighting and good insulation

Pacific Heights Apartment

SAN FRANCISCO, CALIFORNIA, USA **Seidel Architects**

Floor area: 250 square metres / 2700 square feet

Program: Renovation of a 19th-century apartment

Ceiling height/s: 3.3 metres / 11 feet (first level); 3 metres / 10 feet (second level)

Rooms: Entry with curved stair to upper level, living, dining and kitchen with informal seating area, powder room and terrace to garden (first floor); master bedroom suite, guest bedroom, bathroom and office (second floor)

Ventilation: Gas-fired forced-air heating system and operable windows for venting and cooling (San Francisco is a naturally 'air conditioned' climate)

Sound attenuation: The building's structure of large 100-year-old redwood studs, insulation added between floor levels, as well as sound-dampening material on top of existing floors all assist with sound attenuation; additionally, a considerable amount of plywood sheathing was added to interior and exterior walls, improving both seismic and acoustical performance

Green features: New insulation throughout, all-new highly insulated windows with low-E glass and solar shades and high-efficiency water heaters, furnaces and appliances

The character of San Francisco is strongly defined by its trove of historical structures packed onto undulating topography. However, inhabiting a 19th-century residence need not require adopting the conventions and restrictions of Victorian life, as the renovation of this 1894 apartment shows.

The apartment is carved out of a larger four-story structure that was first a large Victorian home, then a hotel, and is now an apartment building. The interior was reconceived from the original typical Victorian layout of small, dark and hyper-discreet rooms into large, light-filled spaces that open one to another and accommodate a contemporary lifestyle.

Glazing to the exterior has been greatly expanded to open up the interiors to a delightful urban garden at the rear of the property. The original 11-foot ceiling works in tandem with the new spatial flow to maximise the sense of volume.

The design consciously juxtaposes a number of modern details with existing historical elements that were preserved and refurbished. For instance, the stark modern fireplace and the curved stairway to the upper level form an interesting contrast with preserved original elements such as crown moldings, bronze hardware, railings and glass panel doors. Contemporary art by Miro, Kelly, and Hockney is mixed with modern furniture of steel, glass and molded plastic and complemented by an occasional antique or primitive art object.

PHOTOGRAPHY: Russell Abraham

152

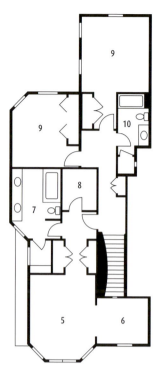

1 Living
2 Dining
3 Kitchen
4 Powder room
5 Master bedroom
6 Alcove
7 Master bathroom
8 Master closet
9 Bedroom
10 Bathroom

Parks Residence

SEATTLE, WASHINGTON, USA | **Eggleston | Farkas Architects**

Credits: Steven Hensel, Hensel Design Studios in Seattle (interior design); Melissa Koch (mural design); dBoone Construction (general contractor)

Floor area: 195 square metres / 2100 square feet (apartment); 19 square metres / 210 square feet (terraces)

Program: Remodel of existing apartment from conventional to loft layout

Ceiling height/s: 2.4 metres / 8 feet (floor slab to ceiling slab—interior concrete to concrete); 2.2 metres / 7 feet 4 inches (at utility soffits)

Rooms: Open loft with living/dining/kitchen/'snug' TV area/office, library/guest suite and utility room

Ventilation: Radiators (building system) concealed by custom panels are supplemented by high-velocity air conditioning integrated into a continuous register at the edge of the soffit

Sound attenuation: Sound-attenuating tile underlay

Located within a 25-year-old high-rise condominium near Pike Place Market, this apartment was formerly a series of small, dated rooms, several of which had large underutilised bay windows. The warren-like entry hallway passed by the master bedroom, kitchen, and bathroom before arriving at the living room. The design was constrained by the fact that the utility chases and soffits, the plumbing drains and the location of the front door could not be changed.

The owners no longer needed multiple bedrooms and bathrooms. Instead, they desired a large flexible space that could be transformed to accommodate catered events and occasional overnight guests. When not entertaining, they wanted their home to feel casual, open and airy.

By removing most of the partition walls, the home was updated to an open, loft-like space stretching 15 metres (50 feet) in length. Replacing conventional doors, floor-to-ceiling pivoting panels allow the space to be transformed. The panels are held in place magnetically and take on the appearance of a finished wall whether open or closed. In this way, guests feel that they arrive through an elegantly panelled entryway rather than a door-filled hallway. Additionally, a rolling panel allows the library to be closed off as a guest suite.

Previously neglected opportunities offered by the building shell were expressed. The concrete columns and ceiling were exposed and cleaned. When a significant imperfection in the concrete above the mural area was discovered during construction, the design was modified and a bent steel plate was added to hide the flaw and provide a custom lighting element for the living-room mural. Each of the window bays gained a new function. In the living area a custom sofa and side platforms were built in. The dining area was furnished with a large steel and wood sideboard. The third bay sports a desk for the home office with file drawers and computer equipment concealed in the rear of the kitchen cabinetry.

PHOTOGRAPHY: Tom Barwick (p. 155 top left/right, bottom left; p. 156 top right; p. 157 bottom left) and Jim Van Gundy (p. 155 bottom right; p. 156 bottom; p. 157 top left to right, bottom right)

1 Entry
2 Kitchen
3 Home office
4 Sitting
5 Dining
6 Living
7 Library
8 Bedroom
9 Dressing room
10 Closet
11 Bathroom
12 Steam room
13 Pantry
14 Utility room
15 Terrace

0   8ft

Playroom Apartment

MOGLIANO, ITALY   **Filippo Caprioglio – Caprioglio Associati Studio di Architettura**

Floor area: 70 square metres / 750 square feet

Program: Conversion of an unused attic space into a child's 'loft apartment'

Ceiling height/s: 2.7 metres / 8.8 feet

Rooms: Bedroom/playroom with closet and art storage space behind inclined dry walls and bathroom

Ventilation: Air-conditioning split system

Sound attenuation: Air-handling unit placed outside to reduce noise

Green features: LED lighting

The idea behind this intervention was to create a playful, flexible and cozy space that was also able to adapt to the changing needs of a growing child. The owners decided that their young son could move into the previously unoccupied attic space connected to their large residence and created an independent 'apartment' for him. The original attic space was dark and the ceiling appeared to be lower than it was due to a series of large and closely spaced structural beams and two large square columns in the middle of the room.

In order to create a multipurpose room without interfering with the original structure, the starting point was the creation of a 'theatre set' of free-form cloud-shaped cuts in a plasterboard wall. The curved shapes of these shelving spaces were inspired by the 1970s French cartoon *Barbapapa* by Annette Tison and Talus Taylor. What might seem a playful or arbitrary gesture was actually carefully considered with regard to the structure, placement and perspective heights of each curvature as well as the precise measurements required to insert the glass shelves within each 'cloud'.

The two central columns were covered with plasterboard and, like the walls, are painted in white to increase the perception of space and provide a neutral background that does not compete with the colours of the child's toys and other belongings. The shelving clouds are lit by tiny LEDs inserted into the structure.

PHOTOGRAPHY: M. M. Archive

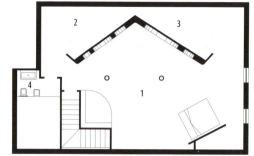

1 Living space
2 Multipurpose zone
3 Closet
4 Bathroom

Pyrmont

PYRMONT, NEW SOUTH WALES, AUSTRALIA **Stanic Harding**

This two-storey penthouse apartment is located in what was originally the boiler house building for a sugar refinery. The boiler house was converted and expanded into a contemporary apartment building by Daryl Jackson Robin Dyke Architects. The client wanted to develop the apartment beyond the basic layout proposed by the developer. This involved a full redesign of the apartment and some necessary alterations to the building structure.

The main public living areas are located on the first level, along with the master bedroom and guest bedroom. The second level accommodates a family room, study, laundry and an expansive roof terrace offering panoramic views of the city and harbour.

The apartment is accessed via a lift that leads directly into an entry space, allowing a controlled separation from the living spaces and the views beyond. The living, dining and kitchen areas are all connected as one space that flows onto the main north-facing terrace. A wood fireplace is located within the lounge and dining area. To extend the connection between the living areas and the external terrace, the window wall was modified to create a clear opening of 8 metres, allowing the apartment to be fully opened to the outside.

A third bedroom connects to the main living area via a large sliding door that parks within the fireplace block. This allows the space to become a more intimate extension of the living area, offering an informal study or reading area.

The kitchen is closely connected to the main public space, however a glazed sliding screen offers privacy when required. The kitchen and related storage form an island within the apartment to separate the master bedroom from the public spaces. A pivot door connecting to the main window wall offers access to the master bedroom and ensuite area. Privacy is obtained as required with another sliding door that can be rolled out of view when not in use.

The open stair visually connects the two levels by means of a combination of voids. The upper level houses a family room and a study area, providing a more private zone for the family to retreat to. The living space on this level connects to the external terrace, which will be developed as an intimate roof garden to accommodate an outdoor kitchen with barbecue facilities.

PHOTOGRAPHY: Paul Gosney

Floor area: 385 square metres / 4100 square feet

Program: A two-storey penthouse apartment within an existing landmark building

Ceiling height/s: Between 2.6 metres and 4 metres / 8 feet and 13 feet

Rooms: Lower level: master bedroom with ensuite, two bedrooms, kitchen, dining, living, bathroom, powder room, terrace; upper level: family room, study, laundry, outdoor kitchen and terrace

Ventilation: Two window walls allow an opening of 8 metres, joining the interior living space to the external terrace and providing cross ventilation

Sound attenuation: Acoustically rated timber flooring

Green features: Intelligent lighting systems

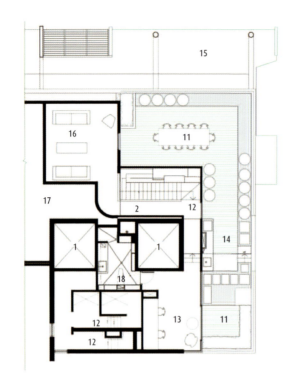

1   Lift
2   Hall
3   Lobby
4   Kitchen
5   Dining
6   Living
7   Bedroom
8   Ensuite
9   WC
10   Store
11   Terrace
12   Stair
13   Study
14   Outdoor kitchen
15   Open to below
16   Family room
17   Plant room
18   Laundry

QUANT 1

STUTTGART, GERMANY **Ippolito Fleitz Group – Identity Architects**

The concept for this model apartment in a converted 1960s laboratory building was to create a living environment that goes far beyond the average and addresses what living is really about: getting the most out of life. Similar to a loft, the apartment is a generous, continuous space. All functions are accommodated in loosely defined areas that can be closed off with sliding doors and heavy curtains if desired. In this way, a whole range of beautifully framed interior and exterior vistas become apparent.

The spacious kitchen, with its freestanding cooking block and expansive dining table, forms the focal point of the apartment. A mirrored ceiling lends impressive definition to the dining area, which is separated from the soft seating landscape by an open room divider. A freestanding wood-burning fire is a source of warmth in the winter. On the south side, the small adjoining library offers a peaceful area for reading or enjoying a relaxed breakfast for two.

The bedroom and study form a common zone defined by oak walls. The dividing wall has integrated sliding doors to connect or separate the two areas, and simultaneously serves as a headrest for the bed and a back to the desk. Behind the bedroom lies the study or guestroom, where a daybed and heavy curtains ensure comfortable quarters for guests.

The concept of the flowing room is supported by an ingenious composition of materials and colours: the elegant, olive green, epoxy resin-coated floor, oak wood surfaces, white varnished finishes, sensuous fabrics and coloured walls engage in an exciting dialogue with one another and, of course, with the occupants.

PHOTOGRAPHY: Zooey Braun

Floor area: 100 square metres / 1140 square feet
Program: Model apartment for a new luxury apartment building
Ceiling height/s: 2.7 metres / 9 feet
Rooms: Gallery with dining, lounge seating areas and attached kitchen area, guest bathroom, bedroom with attached bathroom, coatroom, workroom and guestroom
Ventilation: Natural ventilation and air ventilation of bathrooms
Sound attenuation: Floor and ceiling insulation, open racks and acoustic curtains
Green features: Good insulation, glass with low solar entrée and motor-operated translucent screens for all windows

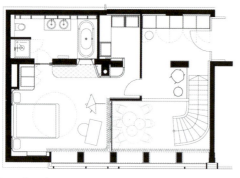

Upper floor plan

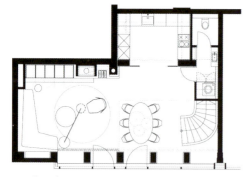

Lower floor plan

Riverside Drive

NEW YORK CITY, NEW YORK, USA **D'Aquino Monaco Inc.**

Floor area: 220 square metres / 2400 square feet

Program: Interior design and architectural remodelling of existing apartment

Ceiling height/s: 3 metres / 10 feet

Rooms: Living, dining, study, two bedrooms with ensuite bathrooms and dressing room, gallery, kitchen, pantry, laundry and powder room

Ventilation: Low-airspeed ceiling plenums

Sound attenuation: Floor and ceiling insulation, acoustically detached walls and acoustically heavily insulated mechanical equipment (also vibration insulated)

Green features: Good insulation, glass with low solar entrée and motor operated translucent screens for all windows

The owners of this Riverside Drive apartment wished to highlight the views of the Hudson River. They expressed a clear desire for a palette of black and white, with a little grey thrown in for good measure. They were ready to make a big change in their lives—and to their living space.

The architect created a kinetic design of sliding lacquered wall panels. Every detail was chosen in a deliberate attempt to create a fluid, reflective space. The river view now provides the colour within this apartment while varying textures of plaster, lacquer and matte surfaces create depth and interest within the almost all-white palette.

A central corridor was removed to allow the living areas to flow into one another and to draw the light and views of the Hudson River further into the space. Spaces are defined by carved poly-laminate sliding doors. The flexibility of the living spaces combined with rich textures and the interplay of matte and polished surfaces create a truly dynamic space that provides a fresh setting for contemporary art and furniture.

PHOTOGRAPHY: Peter Margonelli

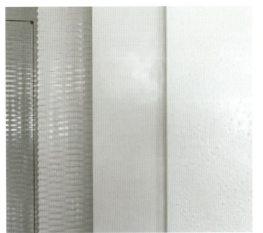

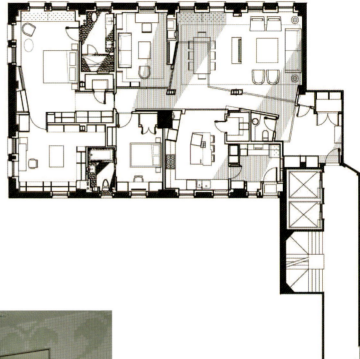

Rosas Apartment

SANTIAGO, CHILE **57STUDIO | Architects**

Floor area: 140 square metres / 1500 square feet

Program: Remodel of a 1930s Art Deco apartment

Ceiling height/s: 2.8 metres / 9 feet

Rooms: Two bedrooms, two bathrooms with family, living and dining spaces, and north and west patios

Ventilation: The southern orientation of the apartment maximises breezes in summer, precluding the need for an air-conditioning system

Green features: Reuse of existing materials such as the wooden floor

This apartment is located in a mid-1930s building in a northwest neighbourhood of downtown Santiago. The design strategy consisted of two main themes: reordering and recovering. The rooms were reordered to adapt the original layout to suit a more contemporary lifestyle. To maximise the living space, it was necessary to tear down only one wall, which incorporated a former secondary bedroom into the large central space. This additional area was transformed into the dining room, thus freeing up space for a family room in the heart of the apartment. An old service bedroom located beside the kitchen was converted into an ample laundry room and storage area. The kitchen was also completely renewed with fresh, contemporary furniture designed by the studio.

The architect went to great lengths to recover most of the original materials typical of a building from this era and well worth preserving. The main goal in this respect was to renew the marvellous original wooden floor, which is composed of a number of different types of Chilean woods. Similarly, the solid wood doors and their original bronze handles were also recovered and given a new lease on life. The owner, an antiques collector with a keen eye for interior design, completed the rest of the decorating and further enhanced this quirky yet stylish apartment.

PHOTOGRAPHY: Caco Oportot

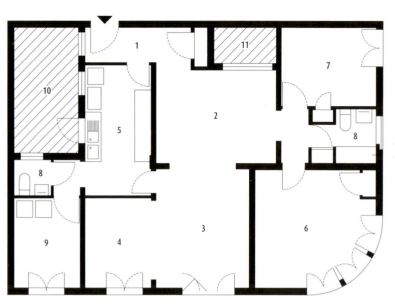

1 Hall
2 Family room
3 Living
4 Dining
5 Kitchen
6 Master bedroom
7 Bedroom
8 Bathroom
9 Laundry
10 West patio
11 North patio

177

S

STUTTGART, GERMANY **Ippolito Fleitz Group – Identity Architects**

Floor area: 95 square metres / 1000 square feet

Program: Apartment and studio for an international graphic designer

Ceiling height/s: 2.7 metres / 9 feet

Rooms: One bedroom with attached dressing room and bathroom, coat room, guest bathroom, gallery with dining and lounge seating areas, workroom, child's bedroom and terrace

Ventilation: Natural ventilation and air ventilation of bathrooms

Sound attenuation: Floor and ceiling insulation, textile coverings of walls, library racks and acoustic curtains

Green features: Good insulation, glass with low solar entrée and motor-operated translucent screens for all windows

The layout of this apartment and work studio is essentially an elongated rectangle with a long hallway on either side connecting the various elements. Two built-in units, each housing a bathroom, give basic structure to the space. As a result, the apartment is divided into clear zones creating private, semi-public and public areas.

In the middle segment of the apartment, the various functional areas are arranged one after another along its entire length. An 'upbeat' is provided by the bedroom, which has direct access to the main bathroom. Opposite this is a guest bathroom. A short connecting corridor running between the two bathrooms marks the vertical borderline of the private area.

Clear-cut cubic forms and the uniform materiality of the smoked oak floor and furnishings establish a calm and uncluttered spatial impression. Colours and textiles are used in different areas as additional atmospheric accents.

The kitchen is located in the very centre of the apartment, an idea that perfectly suits the character of the client. The concrete work surfaces provide a compelling contrast to the wooden kitchen units. Over time, a light patina and slight wear and tear to these surfaces will contribute to the kitchen's charm and vibrancy.

A clear sheet of glass separates the kitchen from the dining area and workspace. The latter consists of a long upholstered bench attached to the back of the freestanding kitchen unit. The space beneath the bench contains two capacious retractable elements at foot level that house a printer and scanner and provide enough storage space for additional work materials. The large dining and work table can be extended to double its size to create a 2-by-3-metre work area.

The rear hallway connects a seating niche with the main bedroom and thus marks the horizontal axis of the private area. It runs along the long strip of glazing, which is contained by a broad windowsill with supports at rhythmic intervals. The rear faces of these supports are painted orange and indirectly lit. At night, a warm orange-red light is reflected back into the room from the windowpanes.

PHOTOGRAPHY: Zooey Braun

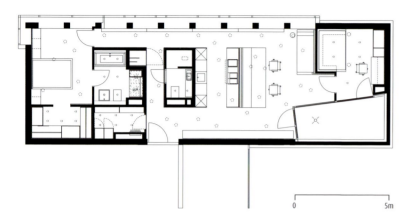

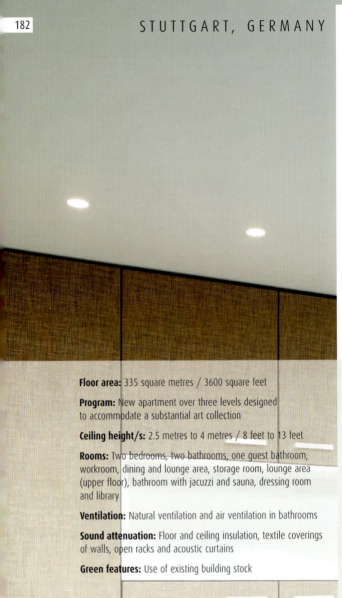

The SCH

STUTTGART, GERMANY

Ippolito Fleitz Group – Identity Architects

Floor area: 335 square metres / 3600 square feet

Program: New apartment over three levels designed to accommodate a substantial art collection

Ceiling height/s: 2.5 metres to 4 metres / 8 feet to 13 feet

Rooms: Two bedrooms, two bathrooms, one guest bathroom, workroom, dining and lounge area, storage room, lounge area (upper floor), bathroom with jacuzzi and sauna, dressing room and library

Ventilation: Natural ventilation and air ventilation in bathrooms

Sound attenuation: Floor and ceiling insulation, textile coverings of walls, open racks and acoustic curtains

Green features: Use of existing building stock

Comprising three mezzanine levels in the upper storeys of a building constructed in the 1980s, this apartment is the result of a rigorous reorganisation of space to create a flowing, three-dimensional room. Its fluid effect is further underscored by light stoneware flooring throughout.

A lift leads directly into the lower floor of the apartment. Here a generous room structured into three areas is revealed. A seating island contained by a luminous circular ceiling and a metal curtain marks the centre of the room and is positioned in front of a long, horizontal window band. The adjacent dining area is characterised by a freestanding, white, high-gloss lacquer kitchen unit. The corridor, along which a wardrobe and row of cupboards are concealed behind a textile skin, leads away from the kitchen towards the private quarters including the study, bathroom and bedroom.

The living mezzanine is accessed from the first landing, where a large, striking mirror opens up the sloping roof and acts as a virtual window. Its oval shape is dissected into four equal parts, which are gently inclined towards the centre and thus produce dramatic and surprising mirror images. The most spectacular eye-catcher of the room, however, remains the remarkable view. It can be properly savoured through the gabled window that opens onto the spacious terrace.

Another landing leads to the top mezzanine, which houses the bedroom and generous bathroom landscape. These two areas are separated by means of a 4-metre glass wall; however, when necessary, an opaque curtain ensures privacy and intimacy in both areas.

The spatial architecture of the apartment is designed entirely around pictures and perspectives. The incredible panoramic views are framed within different settings, and the clients' remarkable collection of paintings creates a striking interplay with the materials, geometric forms and colours of the interior.

PHOTOGRAPHY: Zooey Braun

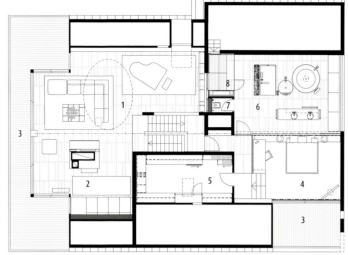

Mezzanine and upper level plan

1 Living
2 Fireplace
3 Balcony
4 Bedroom
5 Dressing room
6 Bathroom
7 Powder room
8 Sauna

Lower level plan

1 Entrance
2 Snooker room
3 Lounge
4 Dining
5 Kitchen
6 Laundry
7 Powder room
8 Bathroom
9 Workroom
10 Bedroom
11 Balcony

0   5m

Seafront Apartment

MALTA   **Architecture Project**

Floor area: 400 square metres / 4300 square feet

Program: Conversion of two large apartments into one massive living space

Ceiling height/s: From 2.2 metres to 2.6 metres / 7 feet to 8.5 feet

Rooms: Common: kitchen, dining, living, gym and hydrobath; private: main bedroom with lounge area, walk-in wardrobe and bathroom, bedroom with ensuite, bedroom with study area and bathroom, guest bedroom and bathroom; utility: laundry, storage and computer room; outdoor: balcony with dining area, balcony with lounge area and balcony with laundry area

Ventilation: Cross ventilation and air-conditioning system

Green features: Double-glazing, cross ventilation, LED lighting and energy-saving light globes and blinds

The challenge presented by this project was to convert two original apartments—characterised by labyrinthine differences in levels, curved steps, colonnade partitions and a compartmentalised plan—into one new open-plan living space.

The typical apartment layout consisting of a corridor with rooms leading off it was discarded and, instead, different spaces were linked together simply by exploiting the flow of natural light. The main living spaces all connect to the central core of the apartment, which houses the kitchen and dining area. This area anchors all of the other main zones: the living quarters, the master bedroom, the second and third bedrooms, and the guest bedroom and utility area.

Continuity was established throughout by creating broad sightlines and expanding openings, allowing the optimum amount of light and ventilation to filter through. Materials and textures play a significant role within the apartment, allowing the positive aspects of the space to be thoroughly optimised. Features such as semi-opaque glass, reflective surfaces and light colours allow light to penetrate every corner of the apartment, while sliding doors and ceiling-high units ensure abundant storage space throughout. The units also act as dividers for the rooms, articulating the space accordingly.

The primary aim of this design was to create a home specific to the clients' needs and tastes and this meant completely rethinking the original space. The new apartment needed to be light, clean, legible and, most of all, an homage to simplicity. The result is a living space in which a dead end will never be encountered. Instead, there is an element of hiding and revealing, a focus on the combination of utility and luxury as well as extreme complexity in the achievement of simplicity.

PHOTOGRAPHY: David Pisani, METROPOLIS

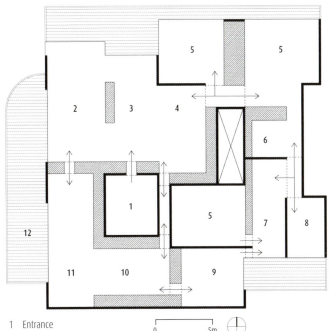

1 Entrance
2 Living
3 Dining
4 Kitchen
5 Bedroom
6 Bathroom
7 Gym/spa
8 Laundry
9 Master bathroom
10 Walk-in robe
11 Master bedroom
12 Terrace

SF Apartment

MESTRE, ITALY **Filippo Caprioglio – Caprioglio Associati Studio di Architettura**

The existing condition and structure of this apartment caused some difficulties during the redesign and construction process—in fact, the entire space revolves around a central pillar, which became pivotal in the spatial reorganisation. This existing structural element influenced the architect to design the entry in direct communication with the living space, which then connects the kitchen—separated only by a large glass wall and door—and a terrace that runs the length of the apartment.

The entry also provides access to the studio and bedrooms via a unique, custom-made system of integrated floor-to-ceiling cabinets, which creates a series of 'secret' rooms. Differences in ceiling height help to expand, stretch and compress the perception of the space, with the assistance of concealed artificial lighting elements.

The fireplace, located next to a niche, was treated minimally to complement the furniture pieces that also contribute to the spatial definition of this elegant apartment.

PHOTOGRAPHY: Athos Lecce

Floor area: 85 square metres / 915 square feet

Program: Renovation of an existing apartment

Ceiling height/s: From 2.4 to 2.7 meters / 8 to 9 feet

Rooms: Living/dining/kitchen, two bedrooms, two bathrooms and terrace

Ventilation: Low-airspeed ceiling plenum and blow-out zone integrated with wall wash lighting armature hidden from main viewing directions

Sound attenuation: Floor insulation, drywall partition with acoustic infill, sound- and vibration-insulated mechanical equipment and air-handling unit placed outside to reduce noise

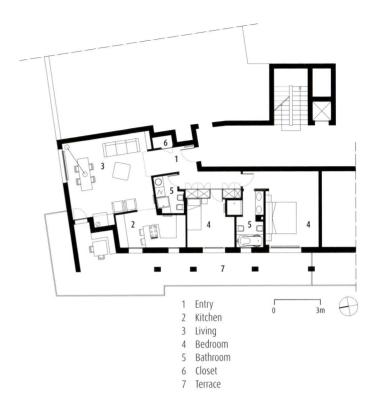

1 Entry
2 Kitchen
3 Living
4 Bedroom
5 Bathroom
6 Closet
7 Terrace

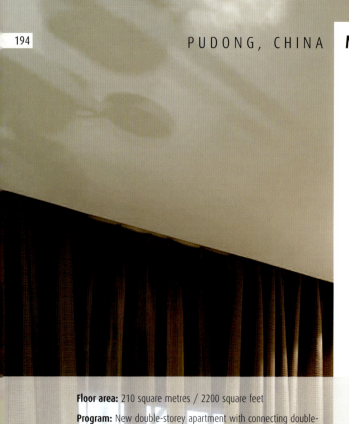

PUDONG, CHINA

Shuwai

MoHen Design International

The double-height terrace of this apartment—located on the seventh and eighth floors of a 20-storey building in Pudong—connects the structure over both floors to give it the appearance of a mini villa inside an apartment building.

On the lower floor the staircase sits like a swivelling hinge for the entire space. It forms part of the striking view from the entrance and acts to divide and define the entire volume into left and right, up and down. A mirror on the ceiling enlarges the hidden vertical cabinetry to the left and right. It also reflects and magnifies the coloured-glass droplight that hangs from the upper floor to the lower floor—the focal point of the apartment—making it 'pop' and shimmer.

To the left of the staircase is the living room, which opens onto the terrace. The ceiling of the terrace is directly connected to the master bedroom on the floor above. Two mirrors in the lower part of the terrace magnify the entire space. To the right of the staircase is the dining room, which connects to the Western- and Chinese-style kitchens. Following the staircase leads to the private area on the second floor, including the master bedroom and secondary bedroom.

PHOTOGRAPHY: MoHen Design International/Maoder Chou

Floor area: 210 square metres / 2200 square feet

Program: New double-storey apartment with connecting double-height terrace

Ceiling height/s: 3.5 metres / 11.5 feet

Rooms: Dining, living, study, master bedroom, master bathroom, guest bathroom and terrace

Ventilation: New central air-conditioning system and dust removal system

Sound attenuation: Floor and ceiling insulation

Green features: Good cross ventilation and use of natural lighting, LED lighting

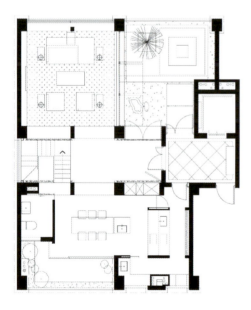

Spring Street Apartment

MELBOURNE, VICTORIA, AUSTRALIA   **Rice Design**

Floor area: 455 square metres / 4900 square feet (including terraces)

Program: Refit of an existing apartment in a former office building

Ceiling height/s: 2.4 to 2.8 metres / 8 to 9 feet

Rooms: Entry: lobby, library, powder room and cellar; common: TV lounge, formal lounge, laundry, kitchen, dining, sitting and terrace; private: guest bedroom suite (bedroom, sitting room, bathroom and balcony) and main bedroom suite (bedroom, study, walk-in robe, ensuite and balcony)

Ventilation: Operable glazing and reverse-cycle air-conditioning system

Green features: Existing windows were replaced with double glazing for more efficient temperature control

Located on the edge of Melbourne's central business district, this apartment building offers fabulous sunrise views over extensive parklands in one direction and sunset views through the city skyline in the other. Originally an office building, it was redeveloped into apartments in the late 1990s. Planned with large, bland, undefined spaces, the standard of the existing interior of this apartment was not commensurate with the location or quality of the space, and the client wished to upgrade the facilities as well as the look.

The complete redesign provided an opportunity to better locate spaces and work within the overall plan to provide facilities in locations that best accentuate their assets. Internal spaces such as the library, cellar and bathrooms are darker and more dramatic, whereas the bedrooms at one end are softer and the living areas at the other end are brighter.

In re-planning, the architect was able to provide the client with three distinct areas within the apartment: public, private and a separate guest area. The entry acts as the hub of the apartment and provides access to all of these spaces, as well as containing the powder room. The master bedroom suite incorporates a dressing area, walk-in robe, ensuite and study.

The refit and re-planning has transformed the apartment into a spacious living environment with a sophisticated edge, where internal areas without access to natural light are used to dramatic effect.

PHOTOGRAPHY: Matt Harvey

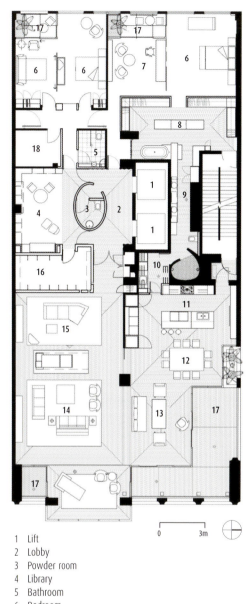

1 Lift
2 Lobby
3 Powder room
4 Library
5 Bathroom
6 Bedroom
7 Study
8 Dressing room
9 Ensuite
10 Laundry
11 Kitchen
12 Dining
13 Casual living
14 Formal living
15 TV lounge
16 Cellar
17 Terrace
18 Storeroom

St. Louis Art House

ST. LOUIS, MISSOURI, USA **Charles Rose Architects**

This penthouse apartment, which occupies the top two floors of a new residential tower in St. Louis overlooking the Mississippi River and the Saarinen Arch, was designed for a couple with a significant contemporary art collection. The clients requested that the design accommodate spaces for both entertaining and the display of their collection.

The design presents museum-quality space with flexible lighting to allow for rotation of the collection. The private elevator hall, entry hall and gallery create a gracious circulation sequence, which delays the impact of the dramatic city views until the visitor either ascends the stairs to the family room and terrace, or enters the living and dining areas. The open spaces of the galleries and living areas contrast with the more-intimate scale of the library and kitchen.

PHOTOGRAPHY: Alise O'Brien

Floor area: 420 square metres / 4500 square feet (apartment); 80 square metres / 900 square feet (terrace)

Program: New apartment combining residential space with larger, more public spaces suitable for entertaining and housing changing exhibitions from the owner's collection

Ceiling height/s: Ranging from 3 metres to 3.4 metres / 9 feet 11 inches to 11 feet

Rooms: Two gallery spaces, living, dining, eat-in kitchen, library, coat room, art storage, family room, terrace, two offices, photo display area, three bathrooms and a master bedroom

Ventilation: Low-velocity system with air vents incorporated into the lighting design

Sound attenuation: All mechanical system elements are on isolation hangers

1 Balcony
2 Living
3 Dining
4 Kitchen
5 Main gallery
6 Entry gallery
7 Library
8 Stair
9 Office
10 Entry
11 Powder room
12 Elevator
13 Laundry
14 Gallery
15 Hall
16 Closet
17 Dressing room
18 Master bathroom
19 Master bedroom
20 Roof garden
21 Terrace
22 Family room
23 Guest bedroom
24 Guest bathroom
25 Photography hall
26 Bar

Upper floor plan

Lower floor plan

St. Ursula Street Apartment

VALETTA, MALTA **Architecture Project**

Floor area: 110 square metres / 1180 square feet

Program: Conversion of two apartments into one in a vertical space with a footprint of 5 by 8 metres and views of the harbour from the upper two floors

Ceiling height/s: Approximately 2.8 metres / 9 feet

Rooms: Hall, master bedroom and bathroom, kitchen, dining room, living room with external terrace and roof terrace accessed via a removable steel stair that also provides shading and storage area above common stairwell

Ventilation: The natural stack effect allows hot air to flow up and out of the roof light and the bedroom, kitchen and living room are cooled by an air-conditioning system

Sound attenuation: Designed as a single space with little need for rooms to be insulated from each other, the shell itself is insulated by double walls and roof insulation

Green features: South-facing glazing is shaded by the removable open-thread steel stair that accesses the roof

A wonderful view of Malta's Grand Harbour can be enjoyed from the back of this three-storey dwelling at the top of an apartment block on the upper side of a stepped street in Valletta. Originally two apartments, these formerly dead spaces were brought to life by adding a floor, developing the living quarters to maximise the views and creating a roof terrace for summer enjoyment.

The creation of an interesting upward-bound route was key to the success of the project. This charming route starts at the front door, located at the top of a traditional winding masonry stairwell. This stairwell typology was used mostly during the English period and is described in Maltese construction vocabulary as *la Ingliza*. At the entrance level the master bedroom and bathroom are discretely tucked away. The internal stairwell is introduced at this level and propels the visitor up toward the light and the views.

The first stop on the upward climb is the marble-clad kitchen, which is aligned with the first sighting of the Grand Harbour as it appears above the rooftops of the buildings of St. Anthony Street at the back. A lightweight steel and glass staircase then leads the visitor up to a lounge that hovers above the entire panoramic sweep of the harbour. A drop-down steel ladder leads up even further to a rooftop terrace located at what is perhaps one of the highest points in Valletta. All of these small yet thrilling spaces exemplify exciting urban living at its best.

PHOTOGRAPHY: Kurt Arrigo

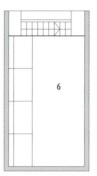
Roof plan

Sixth floor plan

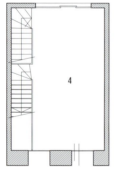
Fifth floor plan

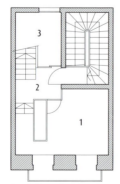
Fourth floor plan

1 Bedroom
2 Hall
3 Bathroom
4 Kitchen/dining
5 Living
6 Roof terrace

Transparent Loft

SEATTLE, WASHINGTON, USA **Olson Kundig Architects**

Credits: Jim Olson, FAIA (design principal, Olson Kundig Architects), Ted Tuttle (interior designer)

Floor area: 240 square metres / 2600 square feet

Program: Entire build-out of a concrete shell, giving the space the openness of a converted loft

Ceiling height/s: From 2.4 metres to 2.7 metres / 8 feet to 9 feet

Rooms: Entrance, dining, living, enclosed kitchen, master bedroom suite with bathroom and walk-in closet, guest bedroom with ensuite, office, powder room and recessed terrace

Green features: Downscaled living and natural ventilation

This 18th-floor condominium in downtown Seattle takes the idea of transparency to its logical extreme. The goal was to improve the boxy proportions of a speculative apartment design to give it the openness of a converted loft. The kitchen and master bathroom are enclosed with walls of glass to match the expanses of glazing on two of the exterior façades and around the recessed terrace. The elevation of the apartment assures privacy, as does the separation of public and private areas with a wall and sliding screen. Rolling blinds can be lowered to protect artworks from glare. When the blinds are raised, especially at night, the city skyline provides a thrilling three-dimensional mural.

The interior design is minimal in materials and palette. A polished black floor sets off the glass and white walls and is warmed by wooden tables, panelling, casework and the soft lines of upholstered seating. In the bathroom, mirrors mounted on the glass walls appear suspended in space—the same illusion is achieved with the metal fittings and sleek cabinetry in the kitchen. The décor provides a neutral backdrop for the owners' collection of life-sized sculptural figures and minimalist paintings.

PHOTOGRAPHY: Benjamin Benschneider

213

TriBeCa Loft

NEW YORK CITY, NEW YORK, USA   **Mojo Stumer Associates, p.c.**

If lower Manhattan beckons modern living, loft space beckons modern design. The harmony of living comfortably among modern artful architecture is the essence of this apartment.

Stainless steel, marble and wood create a cool neutral colour palette. Delineating soffits at multiple heights and a strategic lighting plan create a grand urban environment and give the unusually high ceilings a more human scale.

The clients sought a creative design that simultaneously allowed for open space and created private living areas. The deliberately vast wall space accommodates artwork that has been strategically placed to mimic the function of particular spaces. The railroad layout and high ceilings gave way to unique architecture that plays with length in contrast to height and vice versa.

PHOTOGRAPHY: Paul Warchol

Floor area: 600 square metres / 6500 square feet

Program: Renovated loft apartment over five levels

Ceiling height/s: 3.6 to 7.3 metres / 12 to 24 feet

Rooms: Three bedrooms with full bathrooms, eat-in kitchen, formal living, family room, powder room, formal dining, office, gym, playroom, roof deck and two additional decks

1 Bedroom
2 Bathroom
3 Family room
4 Dining room
5 Kitchen
6 Powder room
7 Living room
8 Storage
9 Gym
10 Media room
11 Office
12 Laundry

Urban Condominium

USA   **Bohlin Cywinski Jackson**

Two art collectors and owners of a 4500-square-foot condominium on a high floor of an urban residential building acquired an adjacent unit, doubling their space to 9000 square feet. They wished to create a comfortable new home, rather than a museum-like environment, in which to enjoy their extraordinary collection.

The architects encountered a number of challenges: awkward spaces, multiple HVAC units at the perimeter, randomly located and immovable shafts, leaking windows, an erratic column layout and low ceilings. The defining strategy was to bring order to the floor plan by creating a clear axial procession through the arrival, public and private spaces. The residence is organised along this axis, leaving the majority of the floor for open planning.

Space configuration, wall geometries and lighting respond to the needs of daily living and socialising in an atmosphere of openness, light and art. Higher ceilings at the perimeter allow maximum daylight penetration. Storage, mechanical and service spaces are located internally. HVAC units were replaced with a dedicated, museum-quality mechanical system, remotely located to improve acoustics and open up dramatic views of the city. Conditioned, humidity-controlled air is supplied between layered ceiling planes.

Upon arrival, the visitor encounters walls sheathed in Sapele wood panelling and slate flooring. Moving inward, rift white oak floors, white plaster walls, a fireplace of Vals Quartzite, and stepped ceiling planes draw the visitor's eyes to the light, the art and the views. The library and den add colour and richness through extensive millwork, bold red accents and richly textured rugs. Bathrooms are appointed in Vals Quartzite, back-painted glass and teak. Careful attention to materiality and detailing achieves a serene and elegant atmosphere where the works of renowned artists enhance life's experiences in very personal ways.

PHOTOGRAPHY: Nic Lehoux Photography

Floor area: 836 square metres / 9000 square feet

Program: Conversion of two condominiums into one large space and accommodation of an extensive art collection

Ceiling height/s: 2.3 metres to 2.5 metres / 7.5 feet to 8 feet

Rooms: Living, dining and family rooms, library, office, den, bar, two guest bedrooms, master bedroom, two wardrobe rooms, kitchen, pantry, laundry, housekeeper's bedroom and mechanical room

Ventilation: Remotely located fan coil system provides heating, cooling and humidity control to the space and new air-cooled chillers were installed to allow for simultaneous heating and cooling as required by the owner's art collection

Sound attenuation: Remotely located fan coil units, roof-mounted air-cooled chillers and sound-engineered drywall-enclosed mechanical room with equipment isolated from structure

Green features: Motor operated translucent screens and low-E coated insulated glazing (PPG Solarban 60)

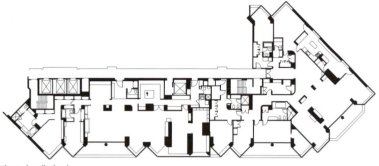

Floor plan (before)

Floor plan (after)

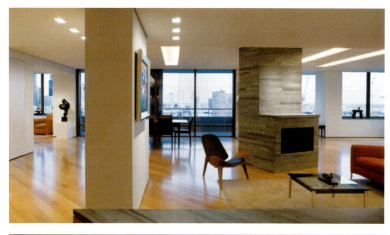

Index of Architects

**57STUDIO	Architects** 57studio.blogspot.com	174	**Craig Steely Architecture** craigsteely.com	70, 106
Adam Richards Architects adamrichards.co.uk	90	**D'Aquino Monaco Inc.** daquinomonaco.com	10, 170
Architecture Project www.ap.com.mt	186, 206	**Damilanostudio Architects** damilanostudio.com	30, 102
Atelier Bugio Arquitectura atelierbugio.com	118	**Eggleston	Farkas Architects** eggfarkarch.com	154
Atelier Peter Ebner and friends ebnerandfriends.com	22	**fmd architects** fmdarchitects.com.au	122
BMA bmarchitecture.com.au	50	**gbc architetti** gbcarchitetti.com	66
Bohlin Cywinski Jackson bcj.com	218	**Harrison Design Associates** harrisondesignassociates.com	114
Caprioglio Associati Studio di Architettura caprioglio.com	62, 82, 158, 190	**Hulena Architects Ltd** hulena.com	86
Carver + Schicketanz Architects carverschicketanz.com	142	**Ippolito Fleitz Group – Identity Architects** ifgroup.org	166, 178, 182
Charles Rose Architects charlesrosearchitects.com	34, 202	**Isay Weinfeld Architect** isayweinfeld.com	18

Johnsen Schmaling	42
johnsenschmaling.com	
marià castelló + josé antonio molina saiz, arquitectes	46
m-ar.net	
McIntosh Poris Associates	54
mcintoshporis.com	
MoHen Design International	146, 194
mohen-design.com	
Mojo Stumer Associates, p.c.	14, 78, 110, 214
mojostumer.com	
ODOS architects	6
odosarchitects.com	
OFIS Arhitekti	130
ofis-a.si	
Olson Kundig Architects	210
olsonkundigarchitects.com	
Peter Kuczia	26
kuczia.com	
Reigo & Bauer	38
reigoandbauer.com	
Rice Design	198
ricedesignstudio.com.au	
RLD	98, 138
www.rldesign.com.au	
Seidel Architects	150
seidelarchitects.com	
Stanic Harding	58, 126, 162
stanicharding.com	
Tham & Videgård Arkitekter	94
tvark.se	
UNStudio	74
unstudio.com	
Zivkovic Connolly Architects	134
zivarch.com	

Every effort has been made to trace the original source of copyright material contained in this book. The publishers would be pleased to hear from copyright holders to rectify any errors or omissions.

The information and illustrations in this publication have been prepared and supplied by the architects. While all reasonable efforts have been made to source the required information and ensure accuracy, the publishers do not, under any circumstances, accept responsibility for errors, omissions, and representations express or implied.